HIKING & BIKING IN THE FOX RIVER VALLEY

HIKING & BIKING IN THE FOX RIVER VALLEY

by Jim Hochgesang

Editing and Nature Notes by Sheryl DeVore
Design by Melanie Lawson
Cover Photography by Jerry Hennen

A Roots & Wings Publication

Dedication

To our children, Jennifer, Julie, and Jeff.
May they do their part to make this planet
a better place for their children.

Created by Sandy and Jim Hochgesang
Offset printing service by Rheitone, Inc.
Printed and bound by United Graphics, Inc.

ISBN 1-884721-05-2

Printed on
recycled paper.

Contents

Acknowledgments

We appreciate the support, input, and guidance of many professionals who reviewed our draft manuscript, provided source maps, and supplied information.

Ders Anderson, Chicago Openlands Project
Greg Behm, George Bellovics, Stacy Miller, Dave Oram,
    Ed Rodiek, and John Schweder, Illinois Department
    of Natural Resources
Bill Donnell, Fox Valley Park District
Jon Duerr and Dick Young, Kane County Forest Preserve District
Mary Eysenbach, Steve Gulgren, Susan Ladendorf, and
    Steve Weller, McHenry County Conservation District
Terry Hannan, Dekalb County Forest Preserve
John Kremer, Boone County Conservation District
Reece Lukei, American Discovery Trail Society
Jean and Paul Mooring, The Illinois Prairie Path
Tom Rickert, Kane County Division of Transportation
Don Sena, Fermilab
Ann Viger, Crystal Lake Park District

A special thanks to the women and men involved in developing and maintaining the trails and pathways in the Fox River Valley and the rest of Chicagoland.

Introduction

Welcome to the fourth in our Chicagoland series of hiking and biking guidebooks. In previous books, we described off-road trails and bicycle paths in Cook, DuPage, and Lake Counties. This guidebook explores the conservation areas, parks, preserves, and pathways farther west in Kane and McHenry Counties. A short time ago, these counties were considered predominately rural/farm country. Now, however, new home developments, businesses, and industries are springing up on what was once cornfields and pastureland as suburbia extends itself. Kane and McHenry Counties are growing rapidly as people move in, drawn to an area with more space and cleaner air in a more rural setting than nearby Chicago. While new developments continue to be built in these counties, you can still find wonderful trails to explore in beautiful natural areas where highway noise fades into the songs of birds and insects and the shimmering wind against tall prairie grasses.

Created by the receding glacier 14,000 years ago, the Fox River headwaters begin in Wisconsin then flow south through the Chain O'Lakes in Lake and McHenry Counties. The river served as a major transportation route as well as a source of food for Native Americans and early settlers who lived along its banks. Today bicyclists, hikers, cross-country skiers, equestrians, in-line skaters, and other trail users enjoy the Fox River Valley's scenic trails. Greenway trails also parallel other Kane and McHenry County streams such as Blackberry and Nippersink Creeks. The Forest Preserve District of Kane County, the Fox Valley Park District, the Illinois Department of Natural Resources, and the McHenry County Conservation District own much of the floodplains along these rivers and streams. These agencies established preserves along the rivers, creeks, and streams where the floodplains escaped development due to nature's propensity to produce spring rain and flooding. As well as providing wonderful places for outdoor recreation, the agencies have helped to improve water quality by restoring wetlands which decrease flooding and absorb pollutants.

The foundation for the trail system in the Fox River Valley is based on several rails-to-trails conversions. The Fox River Trail, the Illinois Prairie Path, the Prairie Trail, the Great Western Trail, and the Virgil Gilman Nature Trail owe their existence to abandoned railroad right-of-ways on which the trails now exist. Often surrounded by remnants of prairie, wetlands, and oak savanna, these greenway trails form an increasingly expanding and interconnected trail system.

Hiking, biking, and cross-country skiing in these natural areas is good for the body, mind, and spirit. A walk through the forest helps put things back into perspective. We are so busy leading our hectic lives and dealing with our many responsibilities. We owe it to ourselves to get away from the computer and the TV. So go take a hike! And bring the family!

How to Use This Guide

You will find a McHenry County map identifying the trail locations on pages 18 and 19 and a Kane County map on pages 20 and 21. Next, notice a summary table listing information such as trail length and type of surface for each site as well as which trails are hiking only.

Following the summary table, 21 sections describe the trails and bike paths starting with the Chain O'Lakes State Park. You'll learn how to get to the site, where to park, what facilities and amenities are available such as bicycle racks, restrooms, and drinking fountains, as well as special information about plants and animals living in or visiting the area. Other attractions such as nature centers are also included.

After the descriptions of the existing trails and bike paths, Section 22 outlines future greenway trail plans throughout Chicagoland and beyond. Section 23 describes the 500+ mile Grand Illinois Trail which will extend from Navy Pier in Chicago to the Mississippi River, then north to Galena before looping back to Chicago. The target is to complete this massive trail system by the year 2000. You can hike and bike much of it today.

Hiking

What we describe as hiking can encompass leisure walking as well as a brisk run. All the trails described in this guidebook are open for hiking.

The trails might have a crushed limestone, asphalt, packed earth, mowed turf, or woodchip surface. As well as being peaceful places to visit, the forests, prairies, and meadows provide the hiker with oxygen given off by the trees and plants rather than the carbon monoxide and other pollutants generated on the streets and highways. And bird songs are better than traffic noise.

Kane and McHenry Counties have trails to meet varying needs. Distances from less than 1 mile to 20 miles or more are available. Tent camping is an option at several sites.

Biking

This guidebook focuses on off-road trails and bike paths. You can bicycle 20, 50, 100, 150, or more miles on interconnected trail systems such as the Fox River Trail, The Illinois Prairie Path, the Prairie Trail, and forest preserves along the way. This guidebook describes how you can get from one trail system to another nearby pathway. In some cases on-road bike routes are described for connec-

On the Fox River Trail in Geneva

tion between two off-road trail systems. If you want to get the cyclist's perspective on the region's street system, the Chicagoland Bicycle Map is an excellent resource. Produced and sold by the Chicagoland Bicycle Federation (CBF), 312-42-PEDAL, the map recommends a regional network of on-street bike routes in addition to showing where the major off-road trails are located. The map does not cover the far western part of Kane and McHenry Counties.

Most asphalt bicycle trails are open for hikers, runners, wheelchair users, and in-line skaters, but not equestrians. Other multi-use trails have either a crushed limestone or gravel surface. Be careful and take it slow.

Mountain biking has become a popular sport. While you won't find any mountains in the Fox River Valley, there are designated trails where a mountain or hybrid bike is more effective than a road bike: for example, the Prairie Trail-Northern Extension in McHenry County or the Great Western Trail in Kane County. In this guidebook we describe which trails are more suitable for mountain or hybrid bicycles. Several conservation areas and forest preserve trails are closed for bicycling to protect the natural areas. Be sure to comply with the trail-use signs at the trailheads.

Cross-country Skiing

When the snow falls, you will find that most of the trails and bike paths described in this book are great places to cross-country ski. The Forest Preserve District of Kane County, the Fox Valley Park District, the McHenry County Conservation District, and the state parks all maintain cross-country ski trails.

Nature Centers

As you hike and bike the Fox River Valley trails, you'll want to stop at the nature centers where the staff as well as brochures and exhibits can help you better understand the ecosystems you will traverse. At nature centers such as Red Oak, Tekakwitha Woods, and the Volo Bog State Natural Area, naturalists present interesting workshops year-round. This guidebook will help you find the centers where you can learn more about the unique programs offered there.

More Information on Programs

Several of the agencies that maintain the trails in the Fox River Valley also offer nature programs and activities year-round. For more information: call the Kane County Forest Preserve District at 630-232-5980. Call the Fox Valley Park District at 630-897-0516. Call the McHenry County Conservation District at 815-678-4431. The three agencies mentioned above also publish quarterly newsletters or activity guides. Telephone numbers for other sites are listed in the individual sections describing those sites.

Rules of the Trail

The popularity of off-road trails continues to grow. As a result, you may encounter bicyclists, runners, wheelchair users, hikers, equestrians, and in-line skaters. Please be courteous and considerate of others so that everyone can enjoy our Fox River Valley trails. Safety suggestions and regulations to protect the environment are described following this section. Please read them carefully. Also some sites have speed limits for bicycles. Check the signage on the trails for any site-specific trail rules.

Nearby Attractions, Bike Shops, Calendar of Events, Organizations

In the appendices, you will find a listing of Fox River Valley area attractions provided by the Aurora, Elgin, and St. Charles Convention and Visitors Bureaus. Included is a listing of bike/skate shops in the area. A monthly calendar of events identifies annual Kane and McHenry County activities. Also included is a listing of environmental, hiking, bicycling, and other related organizations.

While we worked to find as many appropriate events and organization listings as we could, certainly some have been missed. Please notify us of any oversights for future issues. Our address is Roots & Wings, P. O. Box 167, Lake Forest, Illinois 60045.

Comments/Order Form

To improve future editions of *Hiking & Biking in the Fox River Valley*, we would appreciate your comments. A form is on page 159. We'd also like to know if you'd be interested in future guidebooks. Page 160 contains an order form for those who want to purchase additional copies of this book or our other three publications in the Chicagoland series, *Hiking & Biking in Cook County, Illinois*, *Hiking & Biking in DuPage County, Illinois*, and *Hiking & Biking in Lake County, Illinois*.

Rules of the Trail

- Deposit litter in proper receptacles.
- Leave nature as you find it for others to enjoy. Remain on the trail.
- Leash all pets. (Some preserves do not allow pets.)
- Be alert for cars or bicycles.
- Don't feed the wildlife.
- Kane County forest preserves and McHenry County conservation areas are open from 8 a.m. to sunset daily. Call the other sites for hours of operation.
- Don't wear earphones. You can't hear a bicyclist coming.
- Relax, have fun, and enjoy!
- Check for ticks when you're finished.

Specific for Bicyclists
- Wear a helmet.
- Be alert for loose gravel, debris, holes, or bumps on the trails.
- Take it easy with hikers of all ages on the trail.
- Ride in single file.
- Cautiously pass hikers and equestrians on the left. Call out "passing on the left". But remember the hiker may be deaf or hard of hearing or may be wearing earphones.
- Keep both hands on your handle bars.
- Keep to designated bike trails in the forest preserves.
- See "Illinois Bicycle Rules" for additional safety information for on-road bicycling.

For your enjoyment
- Apply insect repellent before you go out depending on the season.
- Take water on long hikes or bike rides.

A Little History

We humans are the most recent addition to the
place on Earth called Chicagoland. Indeed, during the first 99.99 percent of the Earth's life, no
humans were to be found. As recently as 14,000
years ago, ice covered much of what is now Kane
and McHenry Counties. A prolonged warming
climate 11,000 years ago caused the glaciers to
melt, recede, and shape the land. The force and
power of this large glacial movement formed the
beautiful Fox River, the Chain O'Lakes, the
camelback delta kames of Glacial Park, and
many other streams, rivers, moraines, and
kettles that make this area so picturesque.

Soon plants and animals such as the woolly
mammoth, elk, deer, and birds came to live in
this wild area. The first humans to settle in the
Fox River Valley were probably the Paleo Indians.
Their nomadic ancestors had come to North America from Asia via a land bridge. These hunter-
gatherers slowly made their way southward and
eastward. Amateur and professional archaeolo-
gists today still discover spear points in McHenry
County that were used by the Paleo Indians
11,000 years ago. An interesting booklet, "Prehistoric People in McHenry County," published
by the McHenry County Conservation

District, describes an archaeological survey which documented many McHenry County sites where early Native Americans hunted and lived, such as Coral Woods Conservation Area southeast of Marengo.

Milling stones and other artifacts found indicate that between 5,000 and 8,000 years ago, the natives became less mobile as warming and drying continued. Tribes settled in the river valleys which were rich with food sources such as fish, waterfowl, and deer as well as fertile soil for the squash and other crops they planted. In more recent times during the Mississippian Period (450–1,000 years ago), corn became an important part of the Native American's diet as well as buffalo hunted on the prairie in summer. An extensive trade network developed.

In 1673, Father Marquette and Louis Jolliet canoed down the Fox River from what is now Wisconsin searching for a waterway connection between Lake Michigan and the Pacific Ocean. Their visit is the first documented appearance by Europeans into the Fox River Valley. The river they followed was named after the Fox tribe who roamed through the area in the 17th century.

By the time Europeans began settling in the early 1830s, the Native American residents were mostly Potowatami of the Algonquin confederacy of tribes. The early settlers found a grassy sea of prairie with big bluestem and Indian grass growing seven-foot-tall as far as the eye could see. They also discovered a network of Indian trails that crisscrossed the area and supplemented the waterway routes. A few became early wagon routes and subsequently part of today's highway system. For example, the Lake Geneva trail became part of Route 31 and the Belvidere-Waukegan trail lives on today as part of Route 176.

Kane and McHenry Counties were established in 1836. A year later John Deere invented the steel plow which was much more effective for tilling the rich prairie topsoil. Settlers bought land at $1.25 an acre and, very quickly, established a thriving agricultural economy. They built water mills along the Fox River to grind corn and wheat.

In the 1840s, work began on the Illinois and Michigan Canal which was designed to connect Lake Michigan to the Illinois River to provide transport back East for the growing agricultural products of the Midwest and to receive finished goods and products manufactured on the East Coast. Irish, Scottish, and Welsh came from Europe to Kane

Trail of History, Glacial Park

County where jobs were plentiful working on the canal and later the railroads such as the Galena and Chicago Union and the Chicago & Northwestern. By 1860, the communities of Elgin, St. Charles, Geneva, Batavia, and Aurora had all been established. Elgin and Aurora grew into mid-sized cities with much industrial development along or near the river. Today the suburbia of Chicagoland reaches west of the Fox River well into Kane and McHenry Counties with many new home developments, shopping areas, and offices.

Man is the only species with the power to protect or destroy our natural environment. Today the Forest Preserve District of Kane County, the Fox Valley Park District, the Illinois Department of Natural Resources, the McHenry County Conservation District, and other agencies and volunteer organizations are restoring prairies, oak savannas, and wetlands. They hope to preserve open space and natural areas for future generations. At the same time, the agencies are installing new and maintaining existing trails and bike paths. As you hike and bike the wetlands, prairies, and forests on the Fox River Valley trails, please do your part to protect our natural environment.

McHenry County, Illinois Hiking and Biking Trails

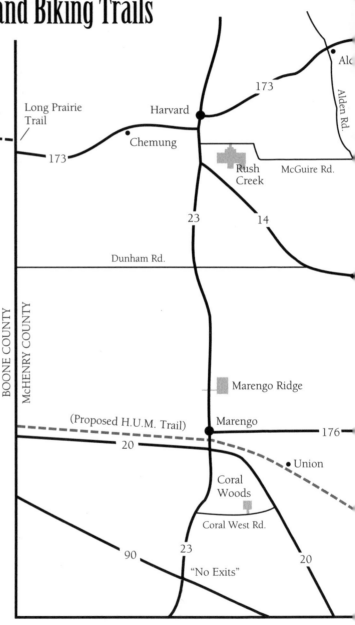

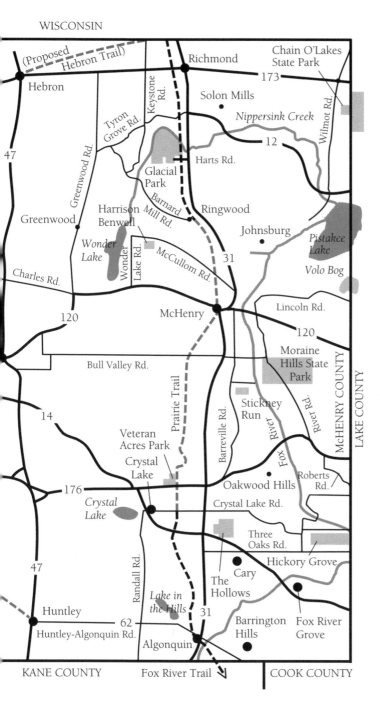

Kane County, Illinois Hiking and Biking Trails

DUPAGE COUNTY

MCHENRY COUNTY

Algonquin

62

Carpentersville

72

25 East Dundee

Tyler Creek Trail

Fox River Trail

Elgin

31

Fox River Shores

West Dundee

Voyagler's Landing

Sleepy Hollow

Tyler Creek

Elgin

Fox River Trail

25

South Elgin

Blackhawk

Fox River

Randall Rd.

Binnie

Binnie Rd.

Gilberts

Big Timber Rd.

Burnidge/ Paul Wolff

20

Udina

Randall Rd.

Galligan Rd.

47

90

Rutland

Pingree Grove

20

47

20

Hampshire

Hampshire

Allen Rd.

72

To Sycamore

Great W.

KANE COUNTY

DEKALB COUNTY

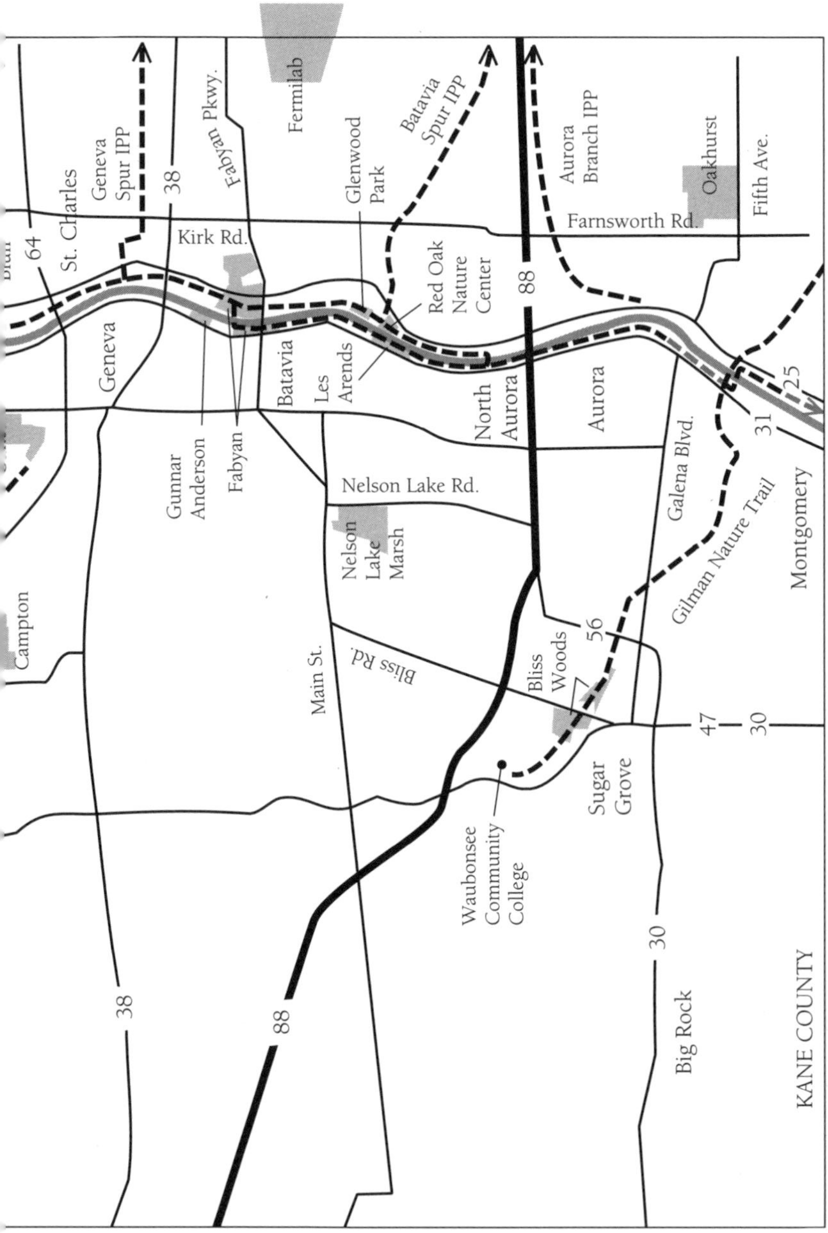
Fermilab
Geneva Spur IPP
Batavia Spur IPP
Aurora Branch IPP
Fabyan Pkwy.
Glenwood Park
Oakhurst
Fifth Ave.
St. Charles
Farnsworth Rd.
Kirk Rd.
Red Oak Nature Center
Geneva
Batavia
Les Arends
North Aurora
Aurora
Gunnar Anderson
Fabyan
Nelson Lake Rd.
Galena Blvd.
Montgomery
Gilman Nature Trail
Nelson Lake Marsh
Campton
Main St.
Bliss Rd.
Bliss Woods
Sugar Grove
Waubonsee Community College
Big Rock
KANE COUNTY
KENDALL COUNTY
64
38
88
56
47
30
31
25

Fox River Valley Hiking and Biking Trails

Park, Preserve, or Trail	Section	Miles—Hike/Bike		Surface	Author's Comments
Chain O'Lakes State Park	1	16.8	6	L, P (See note 1.)	Great place for camping & hiking! Eight miles of equestrian trails open to hikers and cross-country skiers plus 6 miles of multi-use trails and a 2.5-mile nature trail.
Glacial Park	2	6.7	—	M, P	Scenic views from the glacial moraines and kames. Beautiful oak savannas, marshes, bogs, and Nippersink Creek.
Prairie Trail North Extension	3	7.5	7.5	G	Northern section is open to equestrians. Good spot for mountain bikes.
Middle Section		9.7*	9.7*	A	1997 addition will complete the trail from Wisconsin border to Kane County. (See note 2.)
South Extension		8	8	A	Connects to the Fox River Trail.
Volo Bog State Natural Area	4	3.3	—	W,	A .5-mile boardwalk nature trail through the bog and a 2.8-mile loop trail.
Moraine Hills State Park	5	10*	9.5	L	Wetlands, lakes, the Fox River, moraines, and hilly trails offer an excellent place to hike and bike.
Long Prairie Trail	6	14.2	14.2	A	Trail runs all the way across Boone County from the McHenry County border to Winnebago County.
Harvard/Crystal Lake Trail	6	*	*		A 25-mile McHenry County trail proposed from Crystal Lake to the Boone County line. The trail would connect with the Long Prairie Trail and McHenry Prairie Trail as part of the Grand Illinois Trail system.

Park, Preserve, or Trail	Section	Miles–Hike/Bike		Surface	Author's Comments
Eastern McHenry County Conservation District Hiking Trails	7				Trails for hiking and cross-country skiing only.
Harrison-Benwell		2	—	P	Oak, hickory, walnut, and wild cherry trees line the trail.
Hickory Grove/Lyons Prairie & Marsh		5.5*	—	P	Includes a ridge trail through a hickory forest as well as a riverfront path. Separate equestrian trail.
The Hollows		3.6	—	P	Former gravel mining site converted to natural area with some good climbs.
Stickney Run		1.5*	—	M	Oak forest and wetland near the Fox River.
Western McHenry County Conservation District Hiking Trails	8				Trails for hiking and cross-country skiing only.
Rush Creek		3.0	—	P	Favorite spot for bird watching.
Marengo Ridge		3.5	—	P	Hiking and camping in an oak, hickory, and ash forest.
Coral Woods		3	—	P	Maple trees offer beautiful fall colors.
Crystal Lake Trails	9				
Veteran Acres/Sterne's Woods		7	5	P, G	Nature trail through Wingate Prairie and an oak forest.
Winding Creek Bicycle Trail		1.5*	1.5*	A	Bike path through community parks along Woods Creek.
Lippold Park		3.5	3.5	L	Herrick Trail around a marsh and through a new-growth woodland.

Park, Preserve, or Trail	Section	Miles–Hike/Bike		Surface	Author's Comments
Fox River Trail	10	40.6*	40.6*	A	Scenic views of Fox River and adjoining natural areas. One of the premiere trails in Chicagoland.
Tyler Creek Bike Trail		1.2	1.2	A	
River Bend Bike Path		3	3	A, L	
Illinois Prairie Path	11	55	55	L, A	From Kane, through DuPage to Cook County. Four connections with Fox River Trail in Kane County. Country's first great rails-to-trails conversion.
Northern Kane County Forest Preserve Trails	12				Trails for hiking and cross-country skiing only.
Binnie		2.3	—	M	Two mowed turf loop trails.
Rutland		1.2	—	P	Hilly trail through oak grove.
Hampshire		8	—	M	Equestrian trails open for hiking.
Burnidge Forest Preserve	13	9	—	P	Equestrian trails open for hiking. Vehicular and tent camping.
Tekakwitha Woods Nature Center	14	1.3	—	P	Nature center along the Fox River with beautiful wildflowers in the spring.
Great Western Trail	15	17.4*	17.4*	G, L	Rails-to-trails conversion from west side of St. Charles to Sycamore in DeKalb County.
Central Kane County Forest Preserve Trails	16				Trails for hiking and cross-country skiing only.
LeRoy Oakes		1	—	P	Trail along Ferson Creek with high bluff overlook.
Campton		4	—		Equestrian trails open for hiking. Steep descent through oak forest to valley below.

Park, Preserve, or Trail	Section	Miles–Hike	Miles–Bike	Surface	Author's Comments
Fermilab Bike Path and Nature Trails	17	4 / 3.5	4 / —	A, W	Asphalt bike path runs from Kirk Road entrance on west side to Butterfield Road on east side. Connects with Batavia Spur and Aurora Branch of IPP. Woodchip hiking trails through prairies and woods.
Red Oak Nature Center	18	2.7	—	W	Trails through an oak and maple forest along the Fox River and the Fox River Trail.
Southern Kane County Forest Preserve Trails	19				
Nelson Marsh		1.5	—	M	Illinois Nature Preserve west of Batavia.
Oakhurst		1.8	1.8	A, L	Trail around Patterson Lake. Scenic view from large hill. Large wetland and good bird watching.
Virgil L. Gilman Nature Trail	20	14.3*	14.3*	L, A	Through the neighborhoods of Aurora, across the Fox River and along Blackberry Creek, through Bliss Woods to Waubonsee Community College.
Phillips Park, Aurora		2	2	L	Mastadon Trail.
Silver Springs State Fish and Wildlife Area, Kendall County	21	7*	—	M, P	Trails along the Fox River, around Loon Lake, and through a hilly woodland. Extension of the Fox River Trail planned along the river from Oswego to Silver Springs.
Nearby interconnecting trails via Illinois Prairie Path	22				DuPage County Forest Preserves, DuPage County Great Western Trail.
The Grand Illinois Trail	23	500+*	500+*		Currently under development. Will run through 18 counties from Navy Pier to the Mississippi River to Galena back to Chicagoland.

Notes:
1.) Surface designations: A-apshalt, G-gravel, L-crushed limestone, M-mowed turf, P-packed earth, W-woodchip. A mountain or hybrid bike is more effective on a gravel, mowed turf, packed earth, or woodchip trail.
2.) *Signifies additional trails under construction or planned.

Chain O'Lakes State Park

Northwestern Lake County and northeastern McHenry County have by far the largest concentration of lakes in Illinois. The 2,793-acre Chain O'Lakes State Park borders two natural lakes, Lake Marie and Grass Lake. The Fox River flows through the park before it empties into Grass Lake. The river connects eight other lakes that form the chain with over 6,400 acres of water and almost 500 miles of shoreline.

How to get there:

To get to the main entrance from the south take Route 12 north of Fox Lake. Turn right onto Wilmot Road. Continue 2 miles to the park entrance. Coming from the north, take Route 173 and then head south on Wilmot. Be sure to get a map at the ranger station as you enter. The northern area of the park (Oak Point) can be accessed from an entrance on Route 173 just south of the Wisconsin border and west of Channel Lake. The Oak Point day use area has shelters, restrooms, picnic tables, and a canoe/boat launch but no trails.

Pike Marsh at Chain O'Lakes State Park

Chain O'Lakes has one of the best trail systems in the area. You'll discover almost 17 miles of trail including 6 miles of multi-use paths open to bicyclists. The crushed limestone bike trails installed a few years ago have opened up some beautiful portions of the park to trail users. While you can pick up the trail near the entrance or at any of the picnic areas, I suggest driving to the north end of the park road and stopping at the park office. Here you'll find some interesting wildlife displays and a good view of the valley and the Fox River in the distance. The office is open weekdays with Illinois Department of Natural Resources (IDNR) personnel ready to answer your questions. Restrooms, drinking water, and bike racks are available.

The trailhead for the Gold Finch (Yellow) Trail is to the right (west) as you leave the park office. Each of the four multi-use trails has a different color on marking posts along the pathway so you know where you're at—always a good idea! As you walk down the hill from the park office, you'll enjoy six-foot-tall big bluestem and other prairie grasses and wildflowers. The IDNR is restoring the tallgrass prairie that existed here 200 years ago. The 1.7-mile Gold Finch Trail is a loop taking you through a medley of woodlands, open fields, marshes, and along the banks of the Fox River. The river is very wide here. Spring through fall, you may see heron and other waterfowl feeding here, as well as wildflowers blooming nearby. The occasional bench or picnic table provides an opportunity to watch and contemplate.

The path to the right at the first trail intersection will take you back to complete the loop and return to the park office. To continue farther take a left (south) and connect with the Badger (White) Trail. You'll very quickly come to another trail intersection. Take a left onto the Badger Trail, and enjoy the fresh evergreen scent coming from the pine forest. This area is mostly open meadow and prairie covering the rolling hills. The 1.5-mile Badger Trail is also a loop. After about .8 mile there is yet another intersection. The path right will take you north continuing on the Badger Trail to the park office. The path left climbs a hill heading south and interconnects with the Sunset (Orange) Trail. Here you'll find a scenic view to the east of the Fox River and Grass Lake in the valley below.

The 1.7-mile Sunset Trail also includes a short loop. (See map.) To continue south head left past the Hickory Grove Picnic Area. The Sunset Trail winds its way through or near six picnic areas and ends at Catfish Cove near the Maple Grove Boat Launch. At the next trail intersection, the path left takes you first to the Hickory Grove area and then the Pike Marsh North picnic areas. The path right crosses over the park road at the Deer Path picnic area and continues south through the woods. You'll observe a camera symbol sign along the trail with a short woodchip trail down to the marsh. A stick and hay thatched blind has been built by the marsh to watch and photograph waterfowl. After about .5 mile, the trail again crosses over the park road at the Pike Marsh North picnic area. Most of these picnic areas have restrooms and drinking water as well as picnic tables. At Pike Marsh North you'll find a .3-mile trail through woods that is accessible to physically disabled users. A platform overlooks the marsh.

Continue south on the Sunset Trail past the Pike Marsh south picnic area to a trail intersection. The right leg takes you across the park road where the trail ends at Honeysuckle Hollow campground. Beyond that

Chain O'Lakes State Park

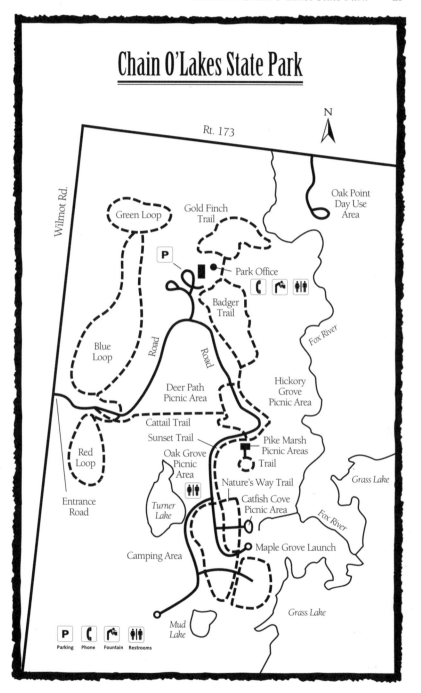

Rt. 173

N

Wilmot Rd.

Oak Point
Day Use
Area

Green Loop

Gold Finch
Trail

P

Park Office

Badger
Trail

Fox River

Blue
Loop

Road

Road

Deer Path
Picnic Area

Hickory
Grove
Picnic Area

Cattail Trail

Sunset Trail

Red
Loop

Oak Grove
Picnic
Area

Pike Marsh
Picnic Areas

Trail

Nature's Way Trail

Grass Lake

Entrance
Road

Turner
Lake

Catfish Cove
Picnic Area

Fox River

Camping Area

Maple Grove Launch

P   C   ⛲   🚻
Parking Phone Fountain Restrooms

Mud
Lake

Grass Lake

lies 44-acre Turner Lake. Farther south you'll find additional camping facilities. Chain O'Lakes is a good spot for a weekend of camping near the trails. The path left takes you farther south through the Oak Grove picnic area where you'll find playground equipment for the kids. Just south of the picnic area is the start of the Nature's Way Trail which is described below. The Sunset Trail ends at the Maple Grove Boat Launch. Concessions, a public telephone, restrooms, and a picnic area are nearby at Catfish Cove. Now it's time to retrace your path back north to the park office.

At the Pike Marsh North Picnic Area, you will come to an intersection you passed earlier heading south. This time take the trail left heading northwest. The Sunset Trail intersects with the newest addition to the Chain O'Lakes trail system. The 1.1-mile Cattail Trail (Brown) spur runs west past the horse corral to the gatehouse near the entrance. Along the way, you will pass a connection to the Red Loop of the equestrian trail. (See below.) You will need to backtrack to the Sunset Trail to continue north. As you enter the Badger Trail north of the Deer Path picnic area, take the pathway left to complete the 6 miles of multi-use trails.

The Nature's Way Trail mentioned above wanders through an oak and hickory forest, runs along a marsh and sedge meadow, and overlooks Grass Lake with its cattail-lined shore. The surface of this 2.5-mile trail is wood chips and packed earth. There are some hills to climb and some nice views. Pick up a Nature's Way Trail Guide at the park office which describes interesting information at eight milestone stops.

Chain O'Lakes also offers 8 miles of equestrian trails on the west side. The trails are open to hikers but bicyclists are not allowed. The northern trailhead is left (west) of the park office. A sign identifies the entrance. The mowed turf trail leads to the east side of the Blue Loop Trail. (See map.) The path right leads north to the Green Loop, a 1.3-mile trail with some of the steepest hiking climbs in Lake County. Most of the trail is packed earth with some gravel. Watch out for the horses coming around sharp curves at the top and bottom of the hills. The Green Loop meanders through deep woods. The 4.7-mile Blue Loop is a mixture of meadow and woods. To the south the Blue Loop leads to the 2-mile Red Loop.

Hikers can access the Red Loop Trail on foot from the Cattail Trail mentioned above. There is limited parking in the horse stable area and behind the gatehouse near the park entrance. The Red Loop trailhead is across the road from the corral. Following the path left, you'll walk along the border of the forest and a prairie. It's very quiet and peaceful here with few highway sounds. As you proceed, the trail enters the woods with steeper hills. You'll enjoy the scenic views along the way.

The park trails are closed for hunting from November to mid-December. In late December, the trails re-open for cross-country skiing, hiking, and biking. The park office serves as a warming station in the winter. Bike and boat/canoe rental is available April through mid-October at the concession area in Catfish Cove. You can also rent tents, cots, and other camping supplies. With 17 miles of trails and extensive camping facilities, Chain O'Lakes is one of the best places in Chicagoland for a weekend of camping, hiking, and biking. Horse rental is available May through October at the corral. Call 847-587-5512 for more information.

Glacial Park

A mere 300 years ago, miles of interlocking wetlands intermingled with rising hills and kames, attracting millions of migrating waterfowl to what is now Glacial Park and surrounding farmland and countryside. Canvasbacks. Redheads. Green-winged teal. Blue-winged teal. Wood Ducks. When these waterfowl species rose from or descended onto the waterways, the earliest humans could see a blend of nature's remarkable hues—powder blue wings, magenta-colored heads, green-crested heads. You can only imagine the sound of these waterfowl stopping in hoards to rest and feed as they headed south for the winter or north to their Canadian breeding grounds.

Drainage tiles laid to aid farmers as well as development destroyed this marvelous habitat. But due to the recent combined efforts of groups such as Ducks Unlimited, the McHenry County Conservation District, the U. S. Fish and Wildlife Service, and

McHenry County Conservation District

Glacial Park

others, Glacial Park visitors can see the ducks once again, not to
mention some state-endangered species including the upland sand-
piper, a bird that makes a most curious whistle as it dances in the air
to attract a mate. Wetland restoration is bringing the ducks back.
Indeed, this area is fast becoming a prime birding spot in McHenry
County.

Glacial Park is one of my favorite places to hike in all of Chicagoland. The landscape at this 2,806-acre conservation area was molded
by the glaciers. You'll wander through or near marshes, prairies
teeming with native grasses, a bog, Nippersink Creek, and unique
camelback-shaped kames created by the accumulation of gravel, sand,
and stone pushed into a hill by the monstrous blocks of ice. At Glacial
Park, you can hike through winding trails among savannas where
giant bur oaks form a canopy over the trail—one of nature's cathe-
drals. You can climb up steep hills to view scenic vistas overlooking
rural farmland, and you can just sit up there, breathing the air,
watching migrating hawks soar over the kames on a cool October day.
Here you can let open spaces soothe your soul.

How to get there:

Take Route 31 north of the town of McHenry or Route 12 south through Richmond to Route 31 south. The McHenry County Conservation District (MCCD) park entrance is on Harts Road west of Route 31. Take Harts Road .6 miles west of Route 31 to the entrance. Parking is available at Wiedrich Education Center north of the entrance or follow the park road around a sharp curve to the kettle parking area east of the marsh. You'll find 6.7 miles of trails here-mostly a combination of mowed turf/packed earth surface with gravel on some of the hills. With the steep climbs and loose gravel and rock on the trails, you will want to wear some fairly sturdy shoes.

From the parking area near the marsh, the 1.2-mile Coyote Trail heads south through a lowland plain along an oak and hickory savanna. The farther you get away from Route 31, the closer you get to natural sounds, breezes across the grasses, and perhaps even the howl of a coyote if you're there early enough in the morning (park opens at 8 a.m). This 44- to 54-inch long mostly nocturnal canine with pointed ears and a light gray body travels through open corridors along edges of woods and bluffs. Move quietly as you enter the trail and you may see this animal which is making a comeback in northern Illinois and others parts of the Midwest.

As you walk the trail, you will pass a large prairie alive in mid-summer with the purple-hued blazing stars, gray-headed coneflowers, and prairie dock, a plant with elephant-sized leaves at the ground upon which a long slender stalk ends in a lovely yellow bloom. The McHenry County Conservation District began restoring this area in 1990.

At the first trail intersection, I headed right toward a large bog. Signs and markers guide the hiker along the way. The bog, a rare ecosystem in Illinois created by glaciers, contains acidic soils making it difficult for plants to obtain water and nutrients. But some unique plants can thrive here. The pitcher plant, for instance, gets its sustenance not from the soil, but from the flies and other insects that get trapped in its sticky cup-like appendages. A boardwalk runs a short distance through the bog for a closer look. If you need a rest, you'll find a bench in the nearby oak savanna overlooking the bog.

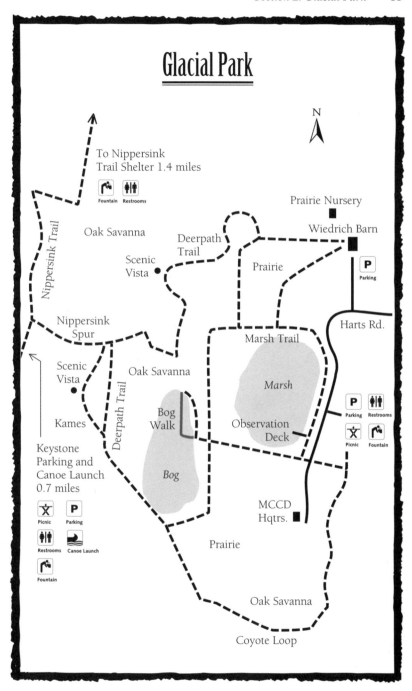

Glacial Park

N

To Nippersink
Trail Shelter 1.4 miles

Fountain Restrooms

Prairie Nursery

Wiedrich Barn

Oak Savanna

Deerpath
Trail

Prairie

P
Parking

Nippersink Trail

Scenic
Vista

Nippersink
Spur

Harts Rd.

Scenic
Vista

Oak Savanna

Marsh Trail

Marsh

Deerpath Trail

Kames

Bog
Walk

Observation
Deck

P   ♦♦♦
Parking   Restrooms

X   ♣
Picnic   Fountain

Keystone
Parking and
Canoe Launch
0.7 miles

Bog

X   P
Picnic   Parking

MCCD
Hqtrs.

♦♦♦   ⚓
Restrooms Canoe Launch

♣
Fountain

Prairie

Oak Savanna

Coyote Loop

East of the savanna is the 1.1-mile Marsh Loop Trail which encircles the marsh area. An observation platform on the east side of the marsh is a good spot to watch the waterfowl visiting the wetlands.

Farther north and west of the marsh is the 2.1-mile Deerpath Trail. You will have a steep climb through a prairie to the Wiedrich Education Center where environmental education programs are offered. Behind the barn is a nursery to grow the prairie plants that are being reintroduced to the land. From the center, the trail heads west to a scenic vista of the valley and Nippersink Creek.

Clearly one of Glacial Park's highlights is the group of kames west of the bog and savanna. The glaciers deposited huge piles of sand and gravel to form large 100-foot-tall hills. The path is narrow here as you climb to the top of the tallest kame. Watch for loose gravel going down and stay on the designated trail to protect the natural wonders from erosion. The walk along the kames was one of my favorites, especially when I was standing higher than the tallest bur oak trees and could see for miles in all directions.

Northwest of the kames is a .2-mile spur that heads west to Nippersink Creek and the 2.1-mile Nippersink Trail. The .7-mile trail to the left (south) crosses over the creek and leads to the Keystone Canoe Launch area. Here you will find water, picnic tables, restrooms and parking along Keystone Road.

The trail to the north leads 1.4 miles along the east bank of the creek. You will pass by a small kame .4 mile to the north at a road crossing. Climb the kame to reach a water fountain in a small oak grove. After crossing a private road the trail heads north for another mile. If you are out on a hot, sunny day, you may want to hike this trail in the afternoon to get some shade from the trees that line the creek. On the way I passed a huge, greenish black turtle, probably a snapper, also out for a hike. Here is a great place to observe wildlife. The creek and wetlands to the east attract turtles, frogs, and birds. A small black-backed hawk called an American kestrel hovered in the air like a helicopter while I was hiking there. It's the kestrel's way of feeding. Hover over your prey, then dive in for the kill. At a trail intersection, cross over the bridge left toward a shelter area. The path to your right is part of the equestrian/snowmobile route. You will find water, a restroom, picnic tables, and a small shelter at trail's end.

With the out-and-back on the Nippersink Trail as well as completing all the loops on the other trails, you will hike about 10 miles. Water, picnic tables, charcoal grills, and restrooms can be found at the kettle parking area east of the marsh. Bring some snacks and a water bottle and spend the day! The trails are open for cross-country skiing in winter. Call the McHenry County Conservation District at 815-678-4431 for information concerning programs and activities.

The largest annual event, "The Trail of History", attracts thousands of visitors to Glacial Park each year in mid-October. The valley west of the kames is transformed into a re-creation of what life was like for the early European settlers. Here you can wander among tents, encampments, and cabins as the sounds of Native American drums, bagpipes, cannons, and muskets fill the air. Adults and children dressed in period costumes demonstrate how to use tools, toys, weapons, and utensils such as a huge iron kettle corn popper. The purpose of the "Trail of History" is to demonstrate how the settlers used the land and its resources and to help us understand that we still use the land today, only in different ways that reflect our culture.

Prairie Trail

Most of the northeastern Illinois rail lines built in the mid-19th Century radiated north, west, and south from downtown Chicago like the spokes of a bike. A few lines, however, ran north and south farther west. A Chicago & Northwestern line ran from Aurora into Wisconsin. The abandoned railroad right-of-way has a new life as home to two of many rails-to-trails conversions throughout Chicagoland. In Kane County, you will find the 41-mile Fox River Trail which runs from Aurora/Montgomery to the Kane-McHenry County line. (See Section 10.) In McHenry County, the South Extension of the Prairie Trail connects with the Fox River Trail and continues north to Crystal Lake. From there, the MCCD plans to complete a 9.7-mile pathway from Crystal Lake north through McHenry to Ringwood to connect with the existing North Extension. When completed, the Prairie Trail will run 25 miles from the Wisconsin border to the Kane County line.

McHenry County Conservation District

On the Prairie Trail

4

North Extension

From the Wisconsin border south to the village of Ringwood, you will find a 7.5 mile gravel trail paralleling Route 31 near the Glacial Park wetlands.

How to get there:

Take Route 31 north of McHenry and south of Richmond to Harts Road. Head west on Harts Road for .3 mile to the trail parking area on the north side of the road.

From the parking area, the trail heads south 2.1 miles to Ringwood. Mountain or hybrid bikes are more effective on the gravel trail which is somewhat bumpy in spots with a lot of equestrian traffic. Glacial Park (Section 2) lies west of the trail offering some scenic views of Lost Valley Marsh. Heading south the trail is elevated most of the way which offers good water drainage on the trail surface. Be very careful crossing School Road with Route 31 traffic exiting a short distance from the crossing.

The trail currently ends at Barnard Mill Road in Ringwood. As mentioned above, the MCCD plans to extend the existing trail 9.7 miles south to Crystal Lake. (See below.) For now, you will need to backtrack to the parking area at Harts Road to explore the rest of the trail.

A very beautiful spot along the path can be found .9 mile north of the parking area at Harts Road. A bridge over Nippersink Creek offers a picturesque view of the creek and the lowland woods along its banks. On a cold day in mid-May, I watched an American goldfinch flit from branch to branch near the bridge, flashing its brilliant yellow and black body. Three and six-tenths of a mile out you will come to the Village of Richmond, known for its antique shops. Another branch of the Nippersink crosses the trail in Richmond.

At 5.4 miles out from the parking area, you will come to the end of McHenry County's Prairie Trail at the state line. A single-track dirt trail continues north for another .3 miles into Wisconsin. Watch out for trees across the path and a steep rocky decline at the end of the trail near a residential area. Barking dogs announce the appearance of any newcomer to the neighborhood.

Prairie Trail

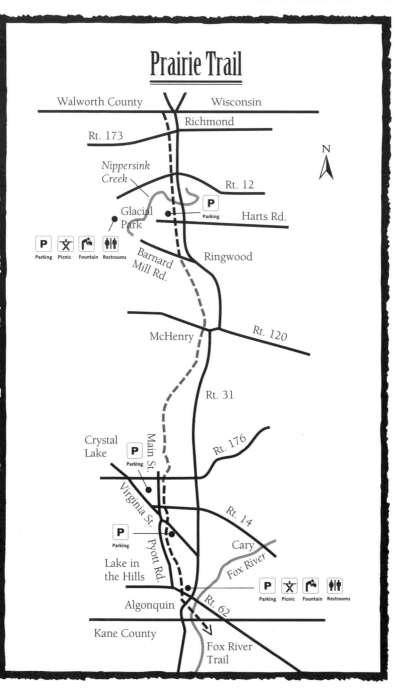

Walworth County — Wisconsin

Richmond

Rt. 173

Nippersink Creek

Rt. 12

N

Glacial Park

Parking [P]

Harts Rd.

[P] Parking   [X] Picnic   [r] Fountain   [♦♦] Restrooms

Barnard Mill Rd.

Ringwood

Rt. 120

McHenry

Rt. 31

Crystal Lake

[P] Parking

Main St.

Rt. 176

Virginia St.

Rt. 14

[P] Parking

Pyott Rd.

Cary

Fox River

Lake in the Hills

[P] Picnic Fountain Restrooms
[P] [X] [r] [♦♦]
Parking Picnic Fountain Restrooms

Algonquin

Rt. 62

Kane County

Fox River Trail

The trail is open to equestrians and to snowmobilers when the snows come. Water and restrooms are available in Glacial Park at the kettle parking lot less than a mile west of the Harts Road parking area. The trail is closed to hiking, biking, and horseback riding when there are four or more inches of snow.

Middle Section

At the time of writing, the MCCD planned to complete a 9.7-mile asphalt trail along the active rail line from Ringwood south through McHenry down to Hillside Road on Crystal Lake's north side.

South Extension

From Crystal Lake south to the Kane County line in Algonquin, you will find 8 miles of asphalt trail. The northern trailhead is in Crystal Lake at Hillside Road; however there is no convenient parking nearby. Good places to park are: 1) the intersection of Virginia Road and Main Street/Pyott Road in Crystal Lake, where you will find a large parking area for trail users, 2) the east side of East Gate Road accessible from Three Oaks Road off of Main Street in Crystal Lake, and 3) a trail ridge parking area accessible from Rt. 62, just east of Pyott Road in Algonquin. This area has both water and restrooms.

How to get there:

Take Route 176 or Route 14 to Crystal Lake. From Route 176, head south on Route 14/Virginia Road. Stay on Virginia when Route 14 veers off left. #1 parking area mentioned above is at the intersection of Virginia and Main Street/Pyott Road next to a bike shop. (See map.) #2 parking area is located along Main Street between Rt. 14 and Pyott Road. #3 parking area is accessed by taking Rt. 31 to Algonquin and heading west onto Rt. 62. Watch for the sign on the right indicating MCCD trail parking. Take the road uphill to the parking area. The pathway on the west side of the area heads downhill to the trail.

At each parking area, you will find an information signpost with a trail map and other information. We will first describe the trail from Virginia Avenue/Pyott Road north to Hillside Road. One and seven-tenths miles run along Main Street paralleling the railroad tracks near shopping areas and an industrial park. The MCCD has recently added additional parking and landscaped a section of the trail here and plans to do more. Also local students are planting native prairie grasses and forbs along the corridor. At Crystal Lake Avenue, the off-road trail temporarily ends. At the time of writing, the MCCD and the City of Crystal Lake planned to designate an on-road bike route north across Route 176 (Terra Cotta Avenue) to Crystal Lake Park District's Veteran Acres Park. (See Section 9.) The latest addition to the Prairie Trail can be found here. A 1.5-mile trail section was added in 1996. Running through Veteran Acres Park and Sterne's Woods, the asphalt pathway is very curvy with steep hills. It's also very scenic. A pine forest lines the trail part of the way. You will need to backtrack south from whence you came until the trail north is completed.

Back at the trailhead at Pyott and Virginia, as you head south, you will come to a mining company's long conveyor belts which are used to transport sand and gravel left by the last glacier. Note the gray mountains over 100-foot-high east of the trail.

Continuing south, the trail becomes more peaceful as it runs through a mature woodland. The asphalt-surfaced pathway is in excellent shape, clean and well-maintained. Approximately 3.3 miles south of Virginia Road, a pathway left of the trail leads up a fairly steep hill to water, restrooms, and a parking area north of Route 62 as mentioned above. Continuing south, a bridge takes you across Route 62. The trail through the community of Algonquin becomes mostly tree-lined with several road crossings at lightly used side streets. Farther south, use the pedestrian button to cross Route 31/Main Street. Two more bridges provide safe crossing over LaFox Street and the scenic Fox River. At 4.8 miles out from the parking area in Crystal Lake, you will come to a sign stating the end of the Prairie Trail at Souwanas Street. Across the street is Kane County and the northern trailhead for the Fox River Trail (see Section 10) which connects with the 55-mile Illinois Prairie Path as well as numerous other off-road trails totaling over 150 miles of interconnected pathways.

The Southern Extension is not open to equestrians or snowmobilers. However, you can cross-country ski in the winter.

Volo Bog State Natural Area

This 869-acre natural area contains bogs, marshes, woodlands, and prairie. East of the town of McHenry, Volo Bog is located in both Lake and McHenry Counties. The entrance, interpretive center, and trails are located a short distance east of the county line in Lake County.

How to get there:

From downtown McHenry, east of the Fox River take Lincoln Road northeast across the Lake County line to Brandenburg Road. Head north on Brandenberg to the entrance. From the east take Route 12 north of Volo. Turn left on Brandenburg Road. The entrance is 1.2 miles west of Route 12.

Volo Bog, one of the state's rarest ecosystems, provides habitat for some 18 Illinois endangered and threatened plants as well as many bird species. This area offers a unique hiking experience providing visitors a glimpse of an Ice Age remnant. Due to its special nature, Volo Bog has been designated as a National Natural Landmark.

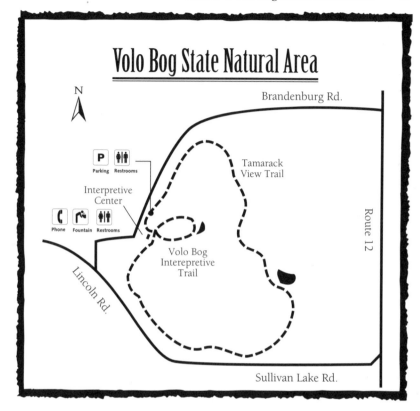

Volo Bog State Natural Area

N

Brandenburg Rd.

Tamarack
View Trail

Route 12

P | Parking   Restrooms

Interpretive
Center

Phone   Fountain   Restrooms

Volo Bog
Interepretive
Trail

Lincoln Rd.

Sullivan Lake Rd.

Stop first at the Visitor Center which was converted from an old
dairy barn. It is open 9 a.m. to 3 p.m. Thursday through Sunday. At
other times, you can find helpful trail guides, maps, and program
listings outside. The preserve is open 8 a.m. to 4 p.m. daily,
September through May, and until 8 p.m., June through August.

You'll find two hiking trails, a short Volo Bog Interpretive Trail, and
the longer Tamarack View Trail, beginning near the Visitor Center.
The self-guiding .5-mile interpretive trail consisting of wooden dock
sections, boardwalk, and a woodchip trail leads you through the bog.
The 47.5-acre bog was originally a deep lake formed by the receding
glacier that subsequently filled with vegetation. Sphagnum moss
formed around the edges and eventually began to cover the entire
lake. Cattails here attract red-winged blackbirds in spring.

The cattails give way to a moss-covered area filled with various ferns including cinnamon, marsh, royal, and sensitive fern, so named because it coils up when touched. Less noticeable are endangered wild orchids that can be found nowhere else in the county.

The trail guide admonishes hikers to stay on the boardwalk since the plants are rooted in a thin mat layer covering 50 feet of water and mucky bog. Halfway around the bog walk is a viewing station where you can listen to frog mating calls in early spring.

Volo Bog, which is on the migratory route for many waterfowl, is a bird watcher's paradise. The best place to see the most birds is on the 2.8-mile Tamarack View Trail. This fairly hilly trail meanders through oak woods, open fields, prairie, and a marsh. Markers are placed at each half mile. On a windy May afternoon, the sea of prairie grasses ripples in the wind like ocean waves.

The trail earns its name from the state-endangered tamarack trees viewed in the distant bog basin. Benches are available along the way. One particularly nice location is near the end of the hike looking down into the bog through the trees. Near the end of the trail, you'll see the pine tree "meeting room" on the left. A narrow trail leads to a conifer grove called the Council of Pines where benches are arranged for programs and presentations. The Tamarack View Trail is open for cross-country skiing in winter when there is a snow base of at least six inches. Bicycling is not allowed on the trails. A bike rack is available to lock up.

The Volo Bog Natural Area is administered by the Illinois Department of Natural Resources. Visitors can enjoy programs and activities year-round. A gift shop run by the Friends of Volo Bog is in the Visitor Center. The Visitor Center is scheduled for upgrades which will make it handicapped-accessible and better suited to all visitors. A quarterly newsletter, "The Bog Log," is available by subscription. Restrooms, drinking water, telephone, and picnic areas are provided. Bring your mosquito repellent during the summer. Call 815-344-1294 for more information.

Moraine Hills State Park

Hiking through the marshes, hills, and forested areas of Moraine Hills State Park, it's difficult to believe that a 2-mile thick glacier once covered the land, and that all that was there was frozen water. No trees. No birds. No humans. But a warming climate brought with it new life, and today we can enjoy the 1,690-acre Moraine Hills, a well-maintained park and one of my favorite places to hike, bike, and cross-country ski. You'll find 800 acres of wetlands here as well as hundreds more acres of savanna, prairie, and open woodland.

How to get there:

Moraine Hills is 2.3 miles southeast of McHenry. From McHenry take Route 120 to River Road (on the east bank of the Fox River). Head south to the park. Take either the McHenry Dam Road to the right (west) to park at the Stratton Lock and Dam along the Fox River or farther south take Main Park

Road to the left. From Route 176 head north on River Road for 3.1 miles to the Main Park Road entrance. You will find nine parking areas along Main Park Road. All have easy access to the trail via short spurs. (See map.)

The multi-use trail system is comprised of three loop trails with a crushed limestone surface. The loop trails are one-way for bicyclists and for cross-country skiers with color codes to identify the path. Trail signage is excellent and precise with distances listed to the hundredth of a mile at each junction (trail intersection). Four junctions A, B, C, and D interconnect the three loop trails. The remaining junctions have the names of the nearby parking/day use areas so it's easy to find your car after a long day on the trails.

On my first visit in early May, I left my car at the first parking area off Main Park Road at Pike Marsh. You'll find water, restrooms, picnic tables, and shelters at all the day use areas. At the time of writing a .7-mile Pike Marsh nature trail north of the parking area was closed for reconstruction. Plans are to reopen the trail including a 1,300 foot floating boardwalk through a marsh in 1998 or 1999.

Access to the 3.7-mile Lake Defiance Trail is west of Pike Marsh across Main Park Road. On the trail along Yellow-Head Marsh, I encountered a family of Canada geese out for a stroll. Waiting for the goslings to clear the trail, I slowly passed by giving the family wide berth. Still I did not escape the protectionistic hissing and raised feathers of one of the parents. Later in the day I met the family again on my way back to the car. This time I got not only hissing and raised feathers, but also a fly by with a slight bump to send me on my way. Bird watchers tell me the best thing to do is proceed slowly and give the family time to clear the trail.

At Junction C, you have two choices. Head right and continue north to the nature center and around 47-acre Lake Defiance or take the trail to the left which heads out to McHenry Dam. If you are on your bike, and plan to take all three loop trails you will end up doing some portion twice because of the one-way loops. This is a nice problem to have in that there is so much to see along the way. Continuing on the gently rolling hills of the Lake Defiance Trail, you will soon come to the park office and nature center. Here you will find

Jerry Hennen

Moraine Hills State Park

Moraine Hills State Park

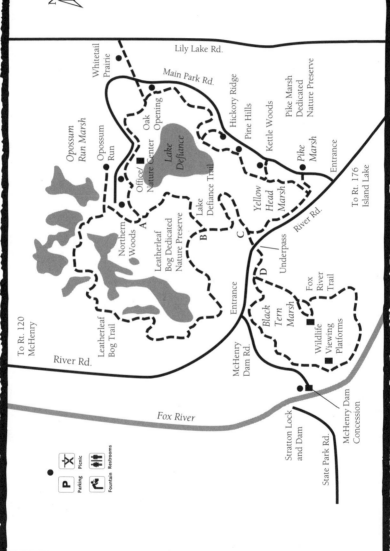

N

Lily Lake Rd.

Main Park Rd.

Whitetail Prairie

Opossum Run Marsh

Opossum Run

Oak Opening

Office/ Nature Center

Lake Defiance

Hickory Ridge

Pine Hills

Kettle Woods

Pike Marsh Dedicated Nature Preserve

Pike Marsh

Entrance

To Rt. 176 Island Lake

Northern Woods

Leatherleaf Bog Dedicated Nature Preserve

Lake Defiance Trail

Yellow Head Marsh

A

B

C

Entrance

River Rd.

D

Underpass

Leatherleaf Bog Trail

Fox River Trail

Black Tern Marsh

Wildlife Viewing Platforms

To Rt. 120 McHenry

River Rd.

McHenry Dam Rd.

Stratton Lock and Dam

McHenry Dam Concession

State Park Rd.

Fox River

Picnic

Parking

Fountain

Restrooms

nature displays as well as a concession stand, bike rack, telephone, and boat rental. There is also a .5-mile self-guided interpretive trail (hiking only) on a boardwalk through the marsh. A free trail guide, available at the park office, describes the flora and fauna along the way.

Walking across this boardwalk early in the morning or near sunset in late March and April might reward you with the strange and eerie winnowing call of the common snipe. This shorebird with large, long, tapered beak announces its intentions to a potential mate by flying high in the air and creating an unusual cascading sound with its wings as it plunges back to earth.

Back on the multi-use trail, the hills become much steeper east of the park office. Take it easy—there are a lot of curves. Also you will probably encounter more trail users on this loop since it connects to all the parking areas. Here you will find scenic views of Lake Defiance and the wooded hills and moraines nearby.

At the Whitetail Prairie junction, take the spur east across the park road to see the prairie restoration. There's also a nice playground area here. The spur ends at the park boundary at Lily Lake Road. Continuing south on the main trail, you will soon return to the starting point at Pike Marsh. Proceed to Junction C to access the 2-mile Fox River Trail. Take the path left which has an underpass beneath River Road. Running along first Black Tern Marsh and then the Fox River, the trail is flatter than the first loop. You will pass an observation area overlooking the marsh. A Wetland Enhancement Conservation Project has helped to bring back waterfowl such as the wood duck, blue-winged teal, and state-endangered black tern.

Stop at the observation area to listen for the unique sounds of the wetland birds that nest here beginning in late April through the end of summer. About 7 a.m. in early May, you will probably hear the rusty hinge-like call of the state-endangered yellow-headed blackbird which lives in denser, wetter cattail areas than its cousin, the red-winged blackbird. Look for this dark bird with the bold coppery yellow head and two chalky, white wing patches visible when it flies. The state-endangered least bittern has also nested here. A master of camouflage, it stretches its long neck, then remains perfectly still so that it blends with the long, slender leaves of the cattails.

The view from the observation deck gives you a picture of the natural ecological succession of an ecosystem. In the middle is open water; just outside are the cattails and other marsh plants. A few willows and cottonwoods are scattered farther out. And behind you are well-established sturdier trees such as maples and oaks. It won't happen during our lifetime, but eventually the entire area could evolve to become a woodland.

At the next trail junction, a short spur heads west through a stand of tall pines to the McHenry Dam. A concession stand, telephone, drinking water, restrooms, picnic tables, playground, and boat rental as well as bait and fishing supplies are available. With the waterfalls at the dam and the wide Fox River, this is another scenic spot. Back on the trail heading south along the river, the path leads along a narrow levee with the river on your right and sloughs on your left. Keep your youngsters in tow along the water. As you head back north to complete the loop, you will encounter another wildlife viewing platform along the marsh.

From Junction D, follow the ABCs in reverse back to Junctions C, B and A. To access the third loop trail head north to the Northern Woods junction. Melting glaciers formed kettles, water-filled depressions covered with sphagnum moss and leatherleaf, as well as the moraines, which refer to the ridges of boulders, gravel, and sand surrounding the kettles. The leatherleaf, a rare plant, has developed a special coating on its leaves enabling it to retain moisture and nutrients. Gleaning moisture and food from a mossy bog is difficult for plants; those that thrive here have evolved to cope with the difficult conditions.

Remember, Moraine Hills is filled with wetlands. Bring mosquito spray in the summer. The trails are open for cross-county skiing in winter. Call the Illinois Department of Natural Resources at 815-385-1624 for more information.

Long Prairie Trail and the Proposed Harvard/ Crystal Lake Trail

In Northwestern McHenry County at the Boone County border, you'll find the trailhead for a 14.2-mile pathway that runs west across Boone County to Winnebago County. The trail was built on an abandoned Chicago & Northwestern (C & NW) railroad right-of-way. A new McHenry County Conservation District trail is proposed to extend from the Long Prairie trailhead at the Boone County line east through Harvard then southeast to Woodstock and on to Crystal Lake where it will connect with the existing Prairie Trail. (See Section 3.) The 25-mile Harvard/Crystal Lake Trail may be built on the right-of-way and parallel to an active commuter line. All three of these trails will be part of the 500+ mile Grand Illinois Trail system planned to loop across northern Illinois from Lake Michigan to the Mississippi River and back. (See Section 23 for more information.) While it will be some time before the proposed McHenry County trail is completed, you can bike or hike the Long Prairie Trail all the way across Boone County today.

How to Get There:

From Route 14/Division Street in Harvard, take Route 173 five miles west through the village of Chemung to County Line Road. Head north on County Line .5 mile to the Long Prairie Trail parking area on the left (west). Parking is also available in the nearby Boone County villages of Capron, Poplar Grove, and Caledonia.

Starting from the eastern trailhead, the well-maintained asphalt surfaced pathway heads west through rural farmland. Nature and historical information is displayed on several signposts along the way. One signpost describes how the Potowatami Indians, having migrated from northern Michigan, made their wigwam homes in the oak savannas that separated forest and prairie.

A bridge near the trailhead crosses Piscasaw Creek which parallels the trail for a bit and crosses back under the trail again farther west. There are many wooden bridges along the way; some very short in wetland areas, others much wider at Beaver and Piscasaw Creeks.

Due to the ubiquity of cornfields across Boone County, the most common trail marker along the Long Prairie Trail is the tractor crossing sign. Two miles from the trailhead, you will pass through the village of Capron. Until 1873 the community was called Long Prairie in recognition of a three-mile long prairie that ran through the settlement southwest to Beaver Creek. Signposts describe the prairie and fen remnants found along the trail west of Capron. A fen is a rare ecosystem in northern Illinois. This small, lowland wet area thrives in cold damp conditions and provides a home to some of the rarest plants in the county. You will also cross "clean and clear" Beaver Creek four times as it meanders along the trail. At 6.5 miles out, is the village of Poplar Grove where tall grain storage bins mark the trail. West of Poplar Grove starting at Route 76 is a recently completed 6.2-mile trail extension that runs through Caledonia to Winnebago County near Rockford. Plans exist to construct a trail heading southwest to nearby Rock Cut State Park and on to Rockford as part of the Grand Illinois Trail.

You will find a restroom and picnic table at the eastern trailhead, but no water. Refreshments are available in the communities along the way but not directly adjacent to the trail. With a 28.5-mile out-and-back, and not much shade, bring water. The trail is open for cross-country skiing in the winter. Call the Boone County Conservation District at 815-547-7935 for more information on the Long Prairie Trail.

Eastern McHenry County Conservation District Hiking Trails

The McHenry County Conservation District offers four sites in the eastern half of the county with interesting hiking and cross-country ski trails.

Harrison-Benwell

Algonquin Indians of the Fox and the Sac tribes hunted deer and other animals here during winter in 18th and early 19th centuries. Later settlers grazed their cattle. In 1973, the Conservation District acquired the 95-acre property.

How to get there:

Take Route 31 (Richmond Road) .6 mile north of Route 120 in McHenry and south of Ringwood to McCullom Lake Road. Head west for 3 miles on McCullom Lake to the conservation area entrance on the left (south) just past Harrison School. Access to the 2-mile Trail of the Big Oaks is southwest of the parking area past the picnic tables and restrooms. The trailhead is at a wooden bridge over a small creek.

The pathway leads through a beautiful forest filled with oak, hickory, walnut, and black cherry trees. These native trees provide copious food for wildlife. Wood ducks, squirrels, and deer eat acorns, walnuts, and hickory nuts in fall and winter. Migrating birds such as thrushes ensconce themselves on cherry trees filling up on the sweet fruits before flying south in fall. Take the time to differentiate between these trees. The hickory has a shaggy, peeling bark with large leaves that turn yellow in fall. The black cherry tree has bark resembling potato chips with smaller leaves. As you pass through the wetland you'll also notice the quaking aspen, named because the leaves seem to quiver in any amount of wind.

You can camp here near the creek, marsh, and oaks. Less than a mile west on McCullom Lake Road is Wonder Lake and the village that bears its name.

Hickory Grove/Lyons Prairie & Marsh

The Fox River meanders along the McHenry/Lake County border south of Route 176 and Fox River Valley Gardens, a small village along the river banks. To the south, near Cary is a conservation area with hiking trails through a hickory and oak forest, as well as wetland and prairie areas near the river.

How to get there:

From the east, take Route 176 west of Wauconda to the village of Island Lake. Head south on Roberts Road for .7 mile. Turn right on Rawson Bridge Road. Head west for 1.3 miles through Fox River Valley Gardens and cross over the Fox River. Turn left at South Rawson Bridge Road. Turn left at Hickory Nut Grove Lane. Proceed .4 mile to the Hickory Grove Highlands entrance on your right. From the west take Route 176 east to Route 31. Head south to Crystal Lake Avenue. Head east to South Rawson Bridge Road. Head left (north) for a short distance to Hickory Nut Grove Lane. Turn right and proceed to the entrance to the Hickory Grove Highlands. (These may be the most complicated directions of any site in our four Chicagoland guidebooks.)

When you find this somewhat secluded spot, you get the trail

Boardwalk through the wet prairie at Hickory Grove

blazer award! But it's worth it with 4 miles of secluded hiking trails. I did not pass one person on my two hikes here. Take the gravel road up the hill to the parking areas. Head right where you'll find a water pump, restrooms, picnic shelter, and tables.

From the trailhead south of the picnic area, the pathway leads into a large hickory and oak forest. A 1.5-mile loop takes you through the woodlands. Signs along the way describe the work of the glacier that sculpted the land. You'll encounter some small hills along the way on this packed earth-surfaced trail. A trail intersection to the right about .7 mile out heads east through a wet prairie. Continuing on the loop trail you will soon come to a 1,330-foot-long boardwalk that leads through the edge of the prairie before re-entering the woods.

The trail intersection on the east side of the loop described above heads west to a road crossing at Hickory Nut Grove Road. This trail leads to the Lyons Prairie & Marsh. Soon you will pass by an oak savanna which is one of North America's rarest ecosystems. At the first trail intersection after crossing the road, the path right leads to another parking area with restrooms and a water fountain. The path

Hickory Grove/Lyons Prairie & Marsh

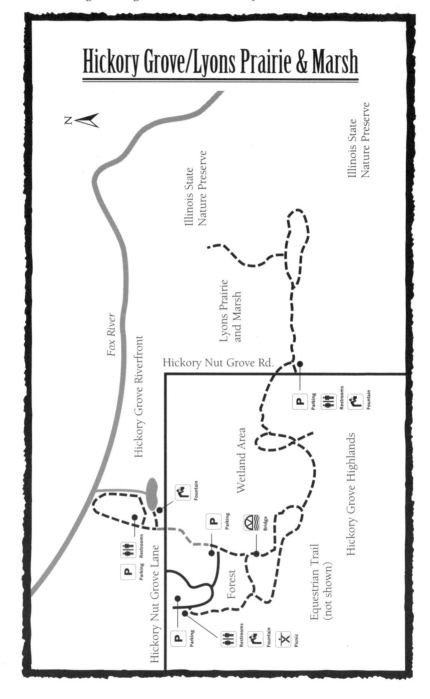

left (east) runs through a beautiful woodland along a ridge. The trail is on a slope here. Stop and soak in the beauty around you. This is a good spot to practice the Native American technique of "still hunting". Quietly stand still, watch, and listen. The traffic sounds are distant if noticeable at all. The bird songs and the wind predominate.

As you continue west, the trail leaves the woodlands and runs through the Lyons Prairie & Marsh, a large part of which is an Illinois State Nature Preserve. Here you will find a 1.6-mile loop through the prairie. A short spur north into the marsh should be completed in 1997. Now the trail ends at a small pond. From here you will need to backtrack to your car.

Across the road from the Highlands parking area is the Riverfront which includes a short trail along the Fox River. The entrance is on the north side of Hickory Nut Grove Lane .1 mile west of the Highlands entrance. The MCCD plans to install a boardwalk through the wetlands connecting the Highlands trail with the Riverfront, a popular fishing spot that connects to the Fox River.

If you cover all the hiking trails, you will have about a 6-mile hike including the backtracking. I found the trail markers at all intersections to be quite helpful. You will find benches along the trail particularly at the intersections. Also there is a separate equestrian trail south of the hiking trail. I talked with a ranger who did not recommend hiking on the equestrian trail since it is usually quite bumpy.

The Hollows

Northwest of Cary and east of Crystal Lake is a 346-acre conservation area called The Hollows. Like so many other natural areas in McHenry County, this site was shaped by the Ice Age. Kames—hills of gravel, boulders and clay—were left behind by the melting glaciers. Wetlands developed in the kettles and lowlands around the gravel hills. The MCCD's research indicates that the land was once used as pasture for dairy cattle.

Gravel and sand mining operations started in 1925 and continued until 1955. In 1977, the conservation district purchased the property and has since begun wetlands restoration. Three miles of trail wind through a cottonwood forest and the hollows or depressions where a half century of excavation left behind high ridges surrounding the giant holes.

How to get there:

Visiting this spot, I found that even McHenry County has traffic jams though nothing like those along the expressways closer to Chicago. Busy Route 14 was being widened to a four-lane road northwest of Cary at the time of writing. Take Route 14 east of Route 31 and .5 mile west of Silver Lake Road. Note the large concrete and stone sign marking the entrance on the north side of Route 14. While quite distinct from the dark wooden signs at most other conservation areas, the megalith serves to define the origins of this place. Follow the entrance road to the parking area east of the ranger residence.

A large trail map on an information signpost north of the parking area depicts the 1.2-mile blue trail and a 1.8-mile orange trail. The trailheads for both are beyond this signpost. The blue trail heads southeast through a hilly woodland area filled with huge cotton-wood trees. A spur off the main trail runs through a hollow out to Lake Atwood. If you need a break, you will find an occasional bench along the way. Good hiking shoes are helpful given the stones, tree roots, gravel, and sand on the trail. Heading back north you will soon come to the connection with the orange trail. The path east is the more interesting. Starting out near a wetland area, you will encounter more large cottonwood trees. There are some rather steep climbs and descents on this trail. Be careful particularly going downhill on the gravel surface. About .6 mile out, you will come to a high bluff overlooking the group camping area. The trail leads downhill east of the campground. The lowland has few trees along the trail but is filled with goldenrod, a native prairie plant, in summer. As you reach the northern-most part of the trail, high ridges on both sides signal the excavations that took place here. Heading back south to the trailhead you will pass by a huge concrete production facility and then West Lake.

A water fountain and restrooms are available at the trailhead. Picnic groves are located near Lake Atwood.

Stickney Run

South of McHenry and west of Moraine Hills State Park is a new conservation area. Stickney Run was opened to the public in November of 1996 as we were finishing this book.

How to get there:

Take Route 31 for 1.6 miles south of Route 120 in McHenry or north from Crystal Lake to Bull Valley Road. Head east .3 mile on Bull Valley to Green Street. Head south on Green (which becomes Barreville Road) for 1 mile to West State Park Road. Head east (left) on West State Park for .3 mile. The entrance is south.

When you visit the newest McHenry County conservation area, you will encounter a wetland in the Fox River floodplain surrounded by rolling hills. A 1.5-mile trail loops through a hilly oak forest and around a pond. Additional trails are planned including boardwalks and nature observation decks which will offer picturesque views of waterfowl visiting the wetland during migration.

The hiking trails at all four sites described above are open for cross-country skiing in winter.

Western McHenry County Conservation District Hiking Trails

Near Harvard and Marengo, you will find three conservation areas with 9.5 miles of hiking trails.

Rush Creek

Located in northwestern McHenry County, Rush Creek is a 550-acre conservation area filled with wetlands, forest, and open meadows near Harvard. Rush Creek, the stream, runs through it on its way southwest to merge with the Kishwaukee River.

How to get there:

Take Route 14 south of downtown Harvard to McGuire Road. Head east on McGuire for .7 mile. The entrance is to the right (south).

The trailhead for three miles of pathways through Rush Creek is located near the parking area south of the pond. The trail leads through a forest filled with hickory, white and red oak, and black cherry trees. A 2.8-mile loop is bisected by a cutback trail in the middle. The terrain is relatively flat. Interpretive signs point out the natural history of the area. This land was first settled in 1835 by the Jerome Family. The woodlands were cut for fuel in the 19th century and during World War I for walnut gun stocks. In 1942, eight acres were set aside as one of the first wildlife conservation demonstration areas. You will see pine trees along the trail that were planted in the 1940s. Around the same time, Rush Creek was channelized to drain the wetlands for farming. The MCCD acquired the land in parcels from 1974 to 1988 and is restoring the wetlands.

Rush Creek is a favorite spot for bird watching. Your best chance of seeing some unusual birds is to head away from the creek to where large stands of white and red oak along with hickory and walnuts grow. Here you'll find large, strong-branched trees that offer prime nesting habitat for large birds of prey such as the great horned owl and the red-tailed hawk. Great horned owls begin nesting in winter, sometimes as early as January; that's when you can hear their deep "Whoo, Whoo, Whoo," calls early in the morning or after dusk. The trees also have hollows and holes where smaller birds such as screech owls and woodpeckers as well as mammals including flying squirrels and raccoons live. Spend some time standing still listening and watching for these beautiful creatures. A walk in middle to late winter can yield some surprising encounters with nature.

You will find a water pump and restrooms, as well as an information signpost at the trailhead. Group camping sites in an oak grove, as well as shelters and picnic areas, are farther west.

Marengo Ridge

North of Marengo is a 325-acre conservation area that welcomes tent campers. There are 3.5 miles of mostly woodland trail along the ridges formed by the last glacier.

How to get there:

Take Route 23 north of Marengo over the Kishwaukee River. The entrance is 1.9 miles north of Route 176 on the east side of Route 23. Once inside the conservation area, turn left at the first auto road intersection and park near the picnic grounds.

Most of the trail can be easily accessed from here. (See map.) Note

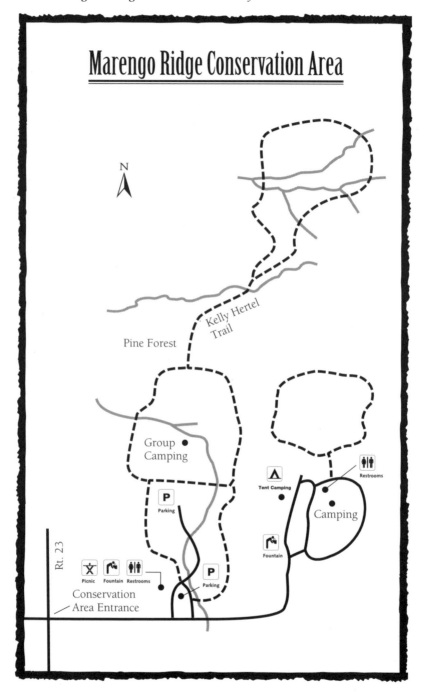

Marengo Ridge Conservation Area

there are two trailheads—one north of the parking area, the other east. A 1.2-mile interpretive trail includes signposts that describe the natural history of the area.

Marengo Ridge is another excellent example of the glacier's work. Here you can hike through an ancient hardwood forest filled with oak, hickory, and ash. Consisting of two adjacent loops, a connecting trail, and a third loop through the northern section of the conservation area, the trail is mostly a packed earth surface with roots and stones. A long steady climb leads north through Kunde Woods with a bridge over a small creek to the Kelly Hertel Trail. A pine forest, planted many years ago, adds diversity to your hike.

After passing through a large open field, you will come to the far northern section of this loop trail which traverses rugged terrain. A small stream, usually dried up in the summer, passes through the woodlands at several spots along the trail. Marengo Ridge is a quiet peaceful spot with little to no traffic sounds most of the way.

Take the east side of the trail loop heading back south where you'll find an impressive evergreen forest filled with red, white, and scotch pine, as well as Norway spruce, Douglas fir, and several other coniferous species. Conifers don't lose all their leaves or needles at once like maples and other deciduous trees do. Instead they gradually lose them throughout the year, making them appear ever green. Their conical shape protects them from winter's wind and snow. Take a close look at their needles to differentiate between them. For example, the native white pine tree has long, flexible needles in groups of five, while the red pine tree needles are in groups of two. Enjoy the fresh scent on a snowy winter day.

The last two interpretive signs describe the impact humans have had on the land. One depicts how a single season of topsoil erosion through clear cutting or farm animal grazing can wipe out thousands of years of nature's work producing fertile topsoil. A quote from Aldo Leopold's 1949 "A Sand County Almanac" posted along the trail is a thought to guide our actions. "We abuse the land because we regard it as a commodity belonging to us. When we see land as a community to which we belong, we may begin to use it with love and respect. There is no other way for man to survive the impact of mechanized man."

Marengo Ridge

Farther east is a .6-mile loop trail north of the camping area. Either drive or hike the auto road to the campground. Here you will find many sites for both tent and RV camping in a beautiful woodland. Call the MCCD for more information about camping at 815-678-4431.

Coral Woods

Three miles of trail near Marengo wind through a peaceful maple forest at the 297-acre Coral Woods Conservation Area.

How to get there:

From Route 23 in Marengo, take Route 20 (Grant Highway) 3.2 miles southeast to Coral West Road. Head west .4 mile to Somerset Drive. Go north (right) on Somerset through a wooded residential neighborhood to the conservation area entrance. The trailhead is on the north side of the parking area.

The path left leads to a 1.2-mile loop nature trail with rugged terrain. The narrow footpath heads west through a meadow and then meanders through maples and along a narrow creek. The trail surface is mostly packed earth with roots, stones, and tree limbs along the way. To the east, a 1.2-mile hiking-ski trail loop is a bit more "civilized." A six-foot-wide mowed turf trail takes you through the rolling terrain of an open meadow and then back into the forest.

The path to the right at the trailhead leads to a .4-mile Maple Sugar Loop Trail which connects to the two longer trails described above. Here you will find the steepest climb at Coral Woods. In the fall, the woodlands are ablaze with orange, red, and yellow leaves. Leaves change colors in response to the shorter amount of daylight and less available moisture as the ground begins to freeze. Then the chlorophyll shuts down to stop photosynthesis. The dominant green color in chlorophyll masks the yellow, red, and orange pigments in the trees. But in fall, it's their time to shine.

A water pump, picnic tables, information signpost, and restroom can be found near the trailhead. Each March the MCCD sponsors The Festival of the Sugar Maples at Coral Woods. Tours are provided as well as a sample of maple sugar collected at Coral Woods. Call 815-678-2219.

The trails at Rush Creek, Marengo Ridge, and Coral Woods are open for cross-country skiing when the snows come.

Crystal Lake Trails

Crystal Lake is a vibrant, fast-growing community in southeastern McHenry County. With all this growth, the community residents decided to preserve a large amount of park land as natural areas and places for outdoor recreation. There are 33 parks spread throughout Crystal Lake. Several have bike paths or trails through or near woodland, prairie, and wetlands maintained by the Crystal Lake Park District.

Veteran Acres Park and Sterne's Woods

The largest natural area in Crystal Lake is composed of two adjoining sites with 7 miles of trails. Veteran Acres Park is north of Route 176 along Walkup Avenue and Sterne's Woods is northeast of the park.

How to get there:

Take Route 176 (Terra Cotta Avenue) west of Route 31 for 1.5 miles to Main Street in Crystal Lake. Turn right (north) to the nature center parking area. The trailhead is to the right of the nature

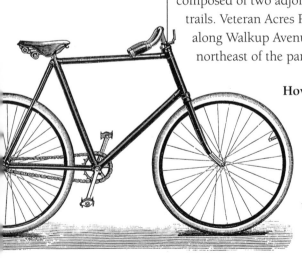

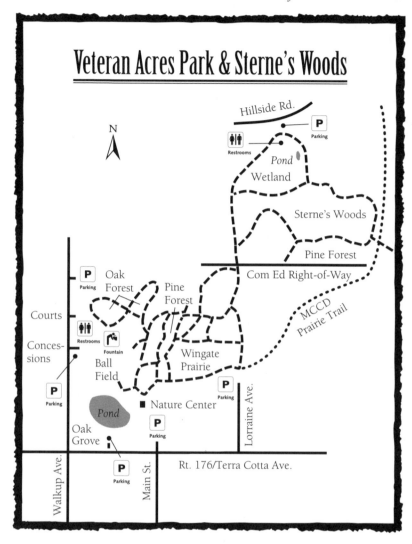

Veteran Acres Park & Sterne's Woods

Hillside Rd.

P Parking

♦♦ Restrooms

Pond

Wetland

Sterne's Woods

Pine Forest

Com Ed Right-of-Way

MCCD Prairie Trail

P Parking — Oak Forest

Pine Forest

Courts

♦♦ Restrooms

Fountain

Conces-sions

P Parking

Ball Field

Wingate Prairie

P Parking

Lorraine Ave.

Pond

■ Nature Center

P Parking

Oak Grove

Walkup Ave.

P Parking

Main St.

Rt. 176/Terra Cotta Ave.

N

center building. Parking is also available at three other locations near the trails. (See map.)

On the east side of Veteran Acres is Wingate Prairie, a 70-acre state nature preserve, named after a volunteer who worked for three decades to restore the forbs and prairie grasses that grew here two centuries ago. Three tall pine groves are surrounded by prairie grasses. Hilly mowed turf trails wind through the prairie. In the northeast

corner of Veteran Acres is a connecting trail to 185-acre Sterne's
Woods which is also a designated Illinois Nature Preserve. Here a 3-
mile gravel multi-use trail loops through pine and oak forests near a
wetland and oak savanna. Narrow hiking-only footpaths off the main
trail wander through the tranquil woods. Markers indicate which
trails are open to bicyclists. A 1.5-mile asphalt addition to the Prairie
Trail described in Section 3 has recently been installed running north
and south through Veteran Acres Park and Sterne's Woods.

On the west side of the 140-acre park, you will find ballfields, a
playground, pond, restrooms, water fountain, and a public telephone. In between is a mature oak forest with hilly hiking and cross-
country ski trails. The trail surface is a mixture of packed earth,
woodchip, and mowed turf. All the trails are somewhat intertwined
with many loops and intersections. Bring a compass to help you find
your way back to your starting point.

Winding Creek Bike Trail

As new home developments spring up in Chicagoland, parks and
bike paths are often installed as part of the initial construction. A
good example is on the south side of Crystal Lake at Woodcreek Park
along Ackman Road. Here you will find a 1.5-mile asphalt bike path,
ballfields, and a huge wooden "Crystal Castle" playground. This is a
good place for young bicyclists or rollerbladers to develop their
skills.

How to get there:

From Route 14 in downtown Crystal Lake, take McHenry Avenue
south 1.8 miles to Randall Road. Turn right on Randall .2 mile to
Ackman Road. Head right (west) .6 mile on Ackman to Golf Course
Road. Turn left. Then take a right on Willow Tree Drive which leads
to a parking area near the bike path.

The bike path runs south of a long pond through Woodcreek Park.
East of Golf Course Road, the path follows Woods Creek south into
Fetzner Park. South of the park a future addition will connect with
an existing path heading south through Winding Creek Park to
Miller Road.

Lippold Park

On the west side of Crystal Lake is a crushed limestone bike path through a large wetland area at 309-acre Lippold Park.

How to get there:

Take Route 176 for .6 mile west of Virginia Street (Route 14). The entrance is to the south.

The park is filled with ballfields and has a free Frisbee golf course as well as the 3.5-mile Walt Herrick Trail which heads west to a marsh and east through a new growth woodland to Green Oaks Road.

Call the Crystal Lake Park District at 815-459-0680 for more information about the parks, activities, and programs offered. Trails at all three sites are open for cross-country skiing in the winter.

Fox River Trail

This is one of the best! Here you'll find the scenic Fox River, a well-designed and well-maintained 41-mile asphalt trail system; many beautiful forest preserves, community parks, and other natural areas; four interconnections with the 55-mile Illinois Prairie Path; and connections with the Prairie Trail, Virgil Gilman Trail, and other pathways and user friendly communities. These blend to make the Fox River Trail, henceforth in the era of acronyms, FRT, one of my favorite trails in Chicagoland. Built on the abandoned right-of-way of two railroad lines, the Chicago, Aurora & Elgin and the Chicago & Northwestern, the trail is the backbone for the Fox River Valley trail system. And each year, thanks to the involved agencies and volunteers, it just keeps getting better!

How to get there:

The FRT runs along or near the Fox from Algonquin to Aurora/Montgomery in Kane County. Routes 31 and 25 parallel the river on or near the west and east river banks. Take whatever east-west road or expressway gets you to the Fox River in Kane County (e.g. I-88, I-90, Routes 20, 30, 38, 56, 62, or 64). You'll find many places along the way to park. Here we'll describe how to get to and where to park at or near the northern and southern trailheads. Throughout this section, we mention some of the other popular and convenient off-road parking areas along the way.

The northern trailhead is at the McHenry-Kane County line in Algonquin at Souwanas Street 1.2 mile south of Algonquin Road/Route 62. There is no convenient off-street parking here. I recommend parking at one of the following three sites: 1) Fox River Shores Forest Preserve on Route 25 two and two-tenths miles south of the county line, 2) The McHenry County Prairie Trail parking area 4.8 miles north of the county line in Crystal Lake at the intersection of Virginia Avenue and Pyott Road. The two trails are continuous and what's another 9 miles or so? 3) A new parking area along the Prairie Trail near Algonquin Road 1.2 miles north of the county line. (See Section 3 for a description of the Prairie Trail.)

The southern trailhead is currently at Illinois Avenue in downtown Aurora on the west bank of the river at McCollough Park. Take Route 25 or Route 31 south of I-88 and north of Route 30 to Illinois Avenue. A bike rack, telephone, water fountain, parking, and restrooms are available at the community center.

Let's take a trip from the McHenry County line south to downtown Aurora/Montgomery then back north to the Fabyan Forest Preserve in Geneva. A round-trip out and back from Algonquin to Aurora is 62 miles. If you add in side trips on the Tyler Creek Bike Trail and the River Bend Bike Path also described in this section, you have a 71-mile trip. Distance traveled from the northern trailhead at the county line is shown as "X miles out." These measurements do not include the side trips described along the way. With connections to the Prairie Trail north, the Illinois Prairie Path east, and other DuPage County trails plus an extension of the FRT south to Oswego scheduled for completion in late 1997, you can explore over 100 miles of additional off-road trails.

For the bicyclists, these off-road trails are not places to try to set land-speed records. The FRT is open dawn to dusk, so take your time

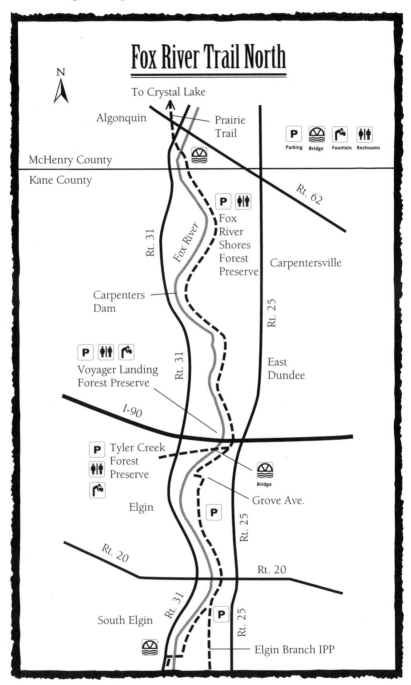

Fox River Trail North

N

To Crystal Lake

Algonquin

Prairie Trail

| **P** Parking | 🌉 **Bridge** | ⛲ **Fountain** | 🚻 **Restrooms** |

McHenry County

Kane County

Rt. 62

P 🚻

Fox River Shores Forest Preserve

Rt. 31

Fox River

Carpentersville

Rt. 25

Carpenters Dam

P 🚻 ⛲

Voyager Landing Forest Preserve

Rt. 31

East Dundee

I-90

P Tyler Creek
🚻 Forest
⛲ Preserve

🌉 **Bridge**

Elgin

P

Grove Ave.

Rt. 25

Rt. 20

Rt. 20

South Elgin

Rt. 31

P

Rt. 25

🌉

Elgin Branch IPP

and enjoy the beautiful natural areas. Be sure to comply with the stop and warning signs along the trail.

I could dedicate this entire book to items of interest along or near the FRT. We will keep the site descriptions brief and focus only on areas that are easily accessible from the trail. In Algonquin, the first mile of the trail leads through a quiet woodland with only one street crossing. After a short on-street segment paralleling Route 31, the trail re-enters the woods near the river. You will come upon a short crushed limestone segment adjacent to the river which encounters frequent washouts during the rainy season. After crossing a creek, you will come to the Fox River Shores Forest Preserve (2.4 miles out). The preserve embraces the river on both banks for a mile and also contains a wetland. Take time to enjoy the wealth of wildlife that uses the river and wetlands. In spring, dozens of species of warblers, tiny insectivorous birds, flit from trees along the river banks catching insects to fatten up before journeying north to the their breeding grounds. The males' brilliant colors are in full glory then. You may see a blue-winged warbler, yellow-rumped warbler, black-throated green warbler, or an American redstart, known as the butterfly of the bird world because it fans out its beautiful black and orange tail. When the lengthening days bring warming sun, painted turtles find a log or other elevated place along the river to sun themselves. These amphibians don't maintain a regulated body temperature like humans, so they need to get their heat from the sun. The wetlands attract migrating waterfowl which nibble on aquatic fish and plants such as duckweed, tiny green plants that float on the surface. In summer, the careful observer may discover water striders, long-legged insects that skim across the water's surface as if it were an ice skating pond. Pack a pair of binoculars in your back pack to use in places like these where the quiet patient human is rewarded with a close view of many interesting animals and plants.

South of the preserve, the trail enters a new growth woods. Note the two long islands filled with evergreen trees. Nearby, the Otto Engineering company is restoring 15 acres of woodland along the river. At 3.5 miles out, you will come to a busy road crossing at Main Street in Carpentersville. The Kane County Forest Preserve District is

restoring a mill race area on the west bank of the river along Lincoln
Avenue at Carpentersville Dam. A nature park with a short trail, picnic
area, and canoe launch was recently opened. A bridge connecting the
nature park with the FRT is planned.

As you enter the community of West Dundee, there are several
crossings at lightly used side streets. South of Barrington Avenue (4.6
miles out) is the Dundee Township Tourist Center on River Street in
East Dundee. Catering to trail users, you will find water, restrooms, a
public phone, snacks & soft drinks, free maps, OUR GUIDEBOOKS,
and other related trail information. Hours are 12 to 4 p.m. weekdays
and 10 a.m. to 4 p.m. weekends from mid-March through October.
Call 847-426-2255 for more information.

Continuing south, you will soon come to the I-90 overpass (6.8
miles out). Under the I-90 auto bridge is a second level bridge for trail
users. For an interesting side trip, take the pedestrian bridge across
the Fox to Voyageur's Landing Forest Preserve. A water fountain,
picnic tables, restrooms, parking, and canoe launch are available to
the right in the forest preserve. The pathway left leads to the 1.2-mile
Tyler Creek Bike Trail. Tyler Creek Forest Preserve has a short hiking
trail through an oak-hickory forest where colorful wildflowers emerge
in the spring. First come the spring beauties with their tiny pink
flowers; next come the anemones with their white blooms, followed
by the taller lavender-hued wild geraniums. These sun-loving wildflowers are called spring ephemerals because they must emerge from
the ground, grow, bloom, and produce seeds before the oak trees leaf
out shading the forest floor. You won't see them in summer, so get out
there in spring to enjoy the show.

Back on the FRT, the next milestone along the way is the city of
Elgin. A water stop and rest area at the Elgin water treatment center
has a scenic view on a bluff overlooking the river. Follow the bike
route sign across railroad tracks to an on-street portion of the trail
starting at Slade Avenue. Turn left and head up the hill to Grove
Avenue. Turn right on Grove (8.3 miles out). Follow the bike route
signs south on Grove for almost a mile to Kimball Street (9.2 miles
out). Cross Kimball at the stoplight. Turn right on the sidewalk south
of the intersection.

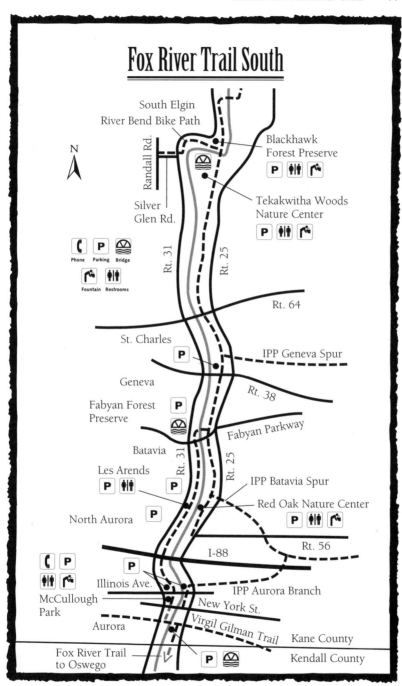

Fox River Trail South

South Elgin
River Bend Bike Path

N

Randall Rd.

Blackhawk
Forest Preserve

P | 👫 | 🚰

Silver
Glen Rd.

Tekakwitha Woods
Nature Center

P | 👫 | 🚰

Phone Parking Bridge

Fountain Restrooms

Rt. 31

Rt. 25

Rt. 64

St. Charles

P

IPP Geneva Spur

Geneva

Rt. 38

Fabyan Forest
Preserve

P

Fabyan Parkway

Batavia

Rt. 31

Rt. 25

Les Arends

P | 👫

P

IPP Batavia Spur

Red Oak Nature Center

P | 👫 | 🚰

North Aurora

P

Rt. 56

I-88

P

Illinois Ave.

IPP Aurora Branch

McCullough
Park

New York St.

Aurora

Virgil Gilman Trail

Kane County

Fox River Trail
to Oswego

Kendall County

P

At the river, turn left and proceed south past the dam. A pedestrian bridge leads out to a small island used by anglers (i.e. politically correct term for fishermen). The FRT continues to the left via an underpass that leads into a parking area along the river. Although not marked, the Prairie Street crossing is the northwestern trailhead for the Elgin Branch of the Illinois Prairie Path (IPP) which coexists on the same route as the FRT for 2.4 miles southeast to South Elgin. This is the first of four trail intersections where the FRT and the IPP interconnect. The FRT continues south past the riverboat gambling casino. A water fountain and air pump are available. There is also a bike rack if you are feeling lucky.

South of the riverboat the trail crosses National Street. The off-road FRT picks up again at 10.5 miles out and heads past some warehouses. Be very cautious passing over the railroad tracks near Raymond Street. The FRT heads back into the woods at Purify Road. After crossing Poplar Creek near where it flows into the Fox, you will come to a major trail intersection at 11.8 miles out. The IPP splits off to the left and heads southeast to Wheaton in DuPage County. A trail parking area is located a short distance to the south on the IPP route. The FRT proceeds to the right heading south along the river under an old stone railroad bridge.

After 12 miles of relatively flat and straight trail, the pathway becomes curvy and hilly. Pay attention to the caution signs. In South Elgin at State Street, the FRT crosses over the Fox River (13.6 miles out). Traveling along the west bank of the Fox, the FRT runs by the Trolley Museum in South Elgin and leads to the Blackhawk Forest Preserve (15.5 miles out). For another interesting side trip at the trail intersection head right into Blackhawk. If you find yourself crossing a bridge back to the east bank, you missed it! Shortly after entering Blackhawk there is a woodchip trail to the right near the river. Here two soldiers who fought in the Blackhawk Indian War of 1832 are buried.

Before you return to the FRT, you may want to extend your side trip. Follow the asphalt trail .4 mile south through Blackhawk to access 3-mile River Bend Bike Path. The trail heads first west and then south past Vasa Park downhill into a wetland. Most of the River Bend

Trail bridge near Blackhawk Forest Preserve

trail is asphalt; however the section through the wetland is crushed limestone. Watch for washouts in the lowland areas. You will find a beautiful spot 1.2 miles out from Blackhawk. A large (by Chicagoland standards) waterfall flows down the dolomite (limestone) creek bed into the wetland. Shortly after the summer deluge of July 1996, the water flow was quite heavy on my first visit. A forest preserve district information signpost describes how fossils from the Silurian Sea hundreds of millions of years ago compressed with mud and calcium deposits to form the limestone we see today. The River Bend trail continues south through the wetland area followed by a long climb up to Route 31 at Silver Glen Road. The bike path continues west on the north side of Silver Glen along an attractive residential neighborhood for .9 mile to Randall Road. A connection south via a bike path along Randall Road is planned to connect with the Great Western Trail (Section 15).

Back on the FRT, the trail crosses over to the east bank of the river via two bridges with a small island in the middle. Here you will encounter the longest climb on the trail. Your reward for conquering the steep hill is beautiful Tekakwitha Woods Nature Center with excellent hiking trails, spring wildflowers, and nature exhibits. See Section 14 for more information. Water, a picnic table, and a restroom are available near the entrance.

Continue south on the FRT along Weber Drive. At Riverwoods Road, the FRT is on-road for .2 mile down a big hill to the Fox River Bluff Forest Preserve. The off-road trail picks up south of the preserve. Dense woods on both sides of the path provide shade and tranquillity. A bridge crosses over Norton Creek near where it empties into the Fox. Following a short distance on-road along Grove Avenue, the trail proceeds between the river on the right and a mature forest to the left. A very picturesque spot!

At 18.9 miles out, the trail climbs a steep hill through the St. Charles Park District's Norris Woods Nature Preserve. Here the trail is a crushed limestone surface. Leaving the preserve, an on-road route proceeds right (south) on 3rd Avenue. Follow the bike route signs for .8 mile past Pottawatomie Park to State Street in St. Charles. Head right (west). Walk your bike down the steep hill to 1st Avenue. You will see the St. Charles Municipal Center across the street. The FRT heads left (south) between the river and 1st Avenue/ Riverside Drive. Use the pedestrian button to cross at Main Street/Route 64 (20.3 miles out).

The off-road trail picks up again at East Illinois Avenue. For another interesting side trip, take the sidewalk on the bridge across Prairie Street. Here you will find St. Charles Park District's Mount Saint Mary's Park. Two miles of asphalt path run along the river to residential areas south of Prairie Street along Route 31 and south through Wheeler Park in Geneva.

Back on the FRT, a historical marker in Langum Park (across Route 25) commemorates the Camp Kane training grounds for the 8th and 11th Illinois Cavalry regiments of the Army of Potomac. The regiment fought in over 50 Civil War battles including Manassas, Vicksburg, and Gettysburg.

South of the park, note the bike route sign which points out a .3-mile "half-loop" up and down a hill through a residential area to avoid biking or hiking along busy and narrow Route 25. After crossing Route 25, the trail enters Good Templar Park. At 21 miles out, a signpost

identifies the connection to the Geneva Spur of the IPP which heads
east up the hill via a switch-back ramp through Good Templar Park.
The FRT is very curvy here through the bottomland along the river.
Also trail usage picks up with more bicyclists, hikers, and in-line
skaters. The path continues through Bennett Park which is a good
parking spot along the river just north of downtown Geneva. The FRT
runs on a sidewalk for a short distance to the State Street/Route 38
crossing. Here is one of the most picturesque spots on this or any
Chicagoland bike trail with a wide dam over the Fox, Old Mill Park,
nearby restored restaurants and shops, and an underpass leading to
beautiful Island Park. One hundred and fifty years ago Bennett Mill
was built here to process flour for the rapidly growing community.
This is a good spot for a break. A bike shop and 3-hour parking is
available along the trail (21.5 miles out).

Take the underpass leading to 11-acre Island Park. In summer the
Geneva Park District's flower gardens add color to this peaceful spot.
Water lilies flourish on a lagoon east of the river. Benches, picnic
tables, a water fountain, public telephones, playground equipment,
and restrooms are available here. At the south end of the park,
another bridge continues your journey south on the FRT.

A short distance south of Island Park is a trail intersection. A
narrow pedestrian bridge crosses the river on a level below a function-
ing C & NW railroad bridge that serves the Metra Line. The Geneva
train station is 7 blocks west if you want to visit the FRT via train.
Hopefully someday soon we will be able to bring our bikes on Metra
to visit Chicagoland's greenway trails rather than always depending on
our motor vehicles. Across the bridge are the forest preserve district's
Gunnar Anderson Sports Fields, a county government center, and a
residential neighborhood.

Continue south on the FRT along the river's east bank. A short side
loop leads through lowland woods along the river. At 22.5 miles out,
in the Fabyan Forest Preserve, notice the 68-foot-tall windmill; built
along York Road in DuPage County in the 1850s, Colonel George
Fabyan had it moved to its present site in 1914. The Colonel and his
wife, Nelle, owned a large estate on the river's west bank. At a trail
intersection, a short distance south of the windmill, a bridge across

Kane County Forest Preserve District

Windmill at Fabyan Forest Preserve

the Fox leads to a beautiful Japanese garden at the former Fabyan estate, the Villa Museum as well as picnic tables, water fountains, bike racks, a trail parking area, and restrooms. Call 630-232-2631 for more information and tour hours. The narrow bridge across the river leads to a continuation of the FRT to the southern trailhead in Aurora. We'll describe that route a bit later. Here the FRT runs south along both sides of the river.

The trail along the east bank is an extension of the Fox River Trail that continues south 5.3 miles to North Aurora at Route 56. Trail signage labels it "Riverside Trail" in a few spots but the pathway is part of the Fox River Trail system.

Let's continue south on the east side to North Aurora. The trail proceeds south first through a dense woods then along Route 25 to the Wilson Street crossing in downtown Batavia (24.1 miles out). Proceed straight ahead for a short distance. Note the trail marker that guides you to the right into a parking area for a restaurant and a bike and outfitters shop. Here is the western trailhead for the IPP Batavia Spur which runs contiguous with the FRT for 1.1 miles. The trail heads into woods along the river south of the parking area. Soon you will come to an amusement park on the south side of Batavia. Proceed through the parking area. At the next trail intersection, the path right leads to the Glenwood Park Forest Preserve. A short distance farther south is another intersection (25.7 miles out). Note the trail signage. Here the IPP-Batavia Spur splits off from the FRT via the path to the left which heads east to Fermilab trails (Section 17) and on to Wheaton via the Aurora Branch. (See Section 11.)

The FRT continues south through a beautiful oak forest. Soon you will come to a large parking area for an archery range. The FRT continues south through the parking lot. Turn right before the railroad tracks for the continuation of the off-road trail. Here the pathway becomes quite hilly and curvy again passing over small creeks and ravines through a mature oak and maple forest. The Fox Valley Park District's Red Oak Nature Center is situated along the FRT (26.9 miles out). There are exhibits at the nature center, interesting hiking trails, and Devil's Cave. This is one of my favorite spots on the trail. Bike racks are available near the entrance. (See Section 18 for more information.)

South of the nature center, the FRT heads downhill to the river and proceeds south on the river's edge for about .3 mile. The trail ends 1 mile south of Red Oak at Route 56 in North Aurora. Highland Park is across the street with parking, a water fountain, picnic tables, and restrooms. If you have followed the trail described without taking any side trips, you have journeyed almost 28 miles from the starting point at the McHenry County line. There is still a lot of the Fox River Trail yet to see on the west bank. To continue, take the sidewalk across the bridge along Route 56. From the intersection on the west side, the trail runs 3.5 miles left to downtown Aurora at New York Street. The path right heads north 4.7 miles to Geneva and the Fabyan Forest Preserve bridge crossing mentioned earlier.

The southbound route runs mostly through shady woodlands leading to downtown Aurora. Along the way, the path crosses under a huge I-88 bridge. At Illinois Avenue, the FRT connects for the fourth and last time with the IPP. The Aurora Branch of the IPP heads northeast to Wheaton. (See Section 11.) A large parking lot for trail users is located on the west bank of the river north of Illinois Avenue. Across the street in McCullough Park, you will find a water fountain, restrooms, a public telephone, bike rack, and parking at the Prisco Community Center. Also located at Illinois Avenue is Veteran's Island and Veteran's Memorial. From Illinois Avenue south to New York Street, bike paths run on both sides of the river near the riverboat casino.

A few blocks south of New York Street, the Virgil Gilman Trail crosses over the Fox and intersects with a new addition to the FRT. From Hazel Avenue at South Broadway Park, a 1.2-mile extension of the FRT runs along the east bank of the Fox from the Virgil Gilman Trail intersection to Mill Street in Montgomery. Parking is available at the trail intersection in South Broadway Park and farther south along Broadway (Route 25). The new trail runs past a scenic dam and on a long peninsula in the river. The bad news is that presently there is no good connection from New York Street to the Virgil Gilman and the new section of the FRT. The good news is that the Kane County Forest Preserve District and the Fox Valley Park District plan to construct a .4-mile off-road trail addition along the river to make the connection. In late 1997 another new addition will take the Fox River Trail south into Kendall County. A 3-mile extension along the east bank of the Fox will begin at Mill Street in Montgomery, currently the southern terminus. The asphalt path will wind along the river to Adams Street in Oswego. Parking will be available in Violet Patch Park near the trailhead. A trail bridge across the Fox will extend to Marina Woods Park along the west bank of the river. Future plans call for further extensions following the river south to Yorkville and on to Silver Springs State Fish and Wildlife Area.

If you are a "through-biker" (stealing a term from the through-hikers who cover the 2,144 miles of Appalachian Trail in one very long hike), there are only 35.3 miles to go to return to the northern terminus at the McHenry County Line. Most of the way, you will be retracing your outbound route, but there is one beautiful stretch of trail we've not yet covered—from Route 56 in North Aurora to the Fabyan Forest Preserve south of Geneva.

To get there head back north along the west bank of the Fox to

Route 56 in North Aurora. An underpass through an old mill race at the Route 56 crossing leads to a long stretch of trail through heavily wooded residential areas along the river. After passing over a small creek, you will soon come to a trail intersection. The path right leads to a .3-mile woodchip hiking trail along the river. A short distance north is another trail intersection leading to Les Arends Forest Preserve south of Batavia. Two hundred years ago, the Potowatami camped here raising corn and beans along the river. Inside a gazebo, information signposts describe some of the history. Captain Dodson and Mr. Clybourn, the first settlers, built a saw mill here in the 1830s. You will also find a nice playground, water fountain, picnic tables, shelters, restrooms, and ample parking along Route 31.

As you head north to Batavia, you will pass by Quarry Beach Swimming Park and Island Park. Entering downtown Batavia, on the west bank of the river, a newly installed brick riverwalk welcomes you. Follow the bike route signs along Shumway Avenue north crossing Wilson Street. Here Shumway becomes Island Avenue. Proceed north for one block. At the time of writing, work was still

Kane County Forest Preserve District

Batavia Dam

underway here on the brick riverwalk. But already it's a beautiful spot. Visit the wildflower sanctuary and large gazebo on a peninsula next to the dam. Along the riverwalk are viewing platforms to watch ducks and other wildlife. Several windmills remind the visitor of Batavia's early history as a leader in windmill manufacturing.

At Houston and Water Streets, you will find the Depot Museum. Built in 1855, the building served as a train station for many years. Today it has a new life as a free museum filled with memorabilia depicting Batavia's history. There is a bike rack available to lock up while you visit the museum. As you leave, be sure to notice the Batavia Riverside Mural of flora and fauna painted on an old building next to the depot. Great blue heron, purple coneflower, and a white birch tree are some examples of the many beautiful nature scenes by local artists.

Soon you will pass under Fabyan Parkway and enter the Fabyan West Forest Preserve described earlier. Cross over the river to return north from whence you came.

The trip described above is almost 72 miles round-trip if you start at the Prairie Trail parking area in Crystal Lake. Adding side trips on the Tyler Creek Bike Trail, the path through Blackhawk, and the River Bend Bike Path, briefly described in this section, bring the total to over 81 miles. With the many existing and planned trail connections with the IPP, Virgil Gilman Trail, and others, the FRT is a gateway to the most extensive trail system in Chicagoland. Enjoy!

The Kane County Forest Preserve District maintains the northern and central segments of the Fox River Trail. For more information call 630-232-5980. The Fox Valley Park District maintains the trail in the Aurora area. Call 630-897-0516 with any questions.

The Illinois Prairie Path

Built on an abandoned railroad right-of-way, this 55-mile trail system runs as a single pathway west from the community of Maywood in Cook County across eastern DuPage County to the Illinois Prairie Path (IPP) focal point in Wheaton. From the Wheaton trailhead, a northwest branch leads to Elgin and a southwest branch runs to Aurora in Kane County. Spurs off the two westbound branches run to Geneva on the northwest route and Batavia on the southwest. Shaped like a sideways rake, the IPP serves as the backbone and connects with many other area trails. As a result, hikers and bikers have access to the most extensive interconnected trail system in the Chicago area.

The Fox River Trail (FRT) connects with the Illinois Prairie Path at four different locations in Kane County with trail intersections in Elgin, Geneva, Batavia, and Aurora. (See map.) Thanks to

these two backbone systems, trail users can access over 150 miles of off-road trails and bike paths in Cook, DuPage, Kane, and McHenry Counties.

The IPP was built on the roadbed of the Chicago, Aurora, and Elgin Railroad (C.A.& E.), an electric line that served the western suburbs for 60 years from 1902 to 1961. A naturalist at The Morton Arboretum, May Theilgaard Watts, suggested turning the abandoned roadbed into a path system where people could walk and bicycle through natural areas. Watts, a teacher and an author of books and poems detailing the natural history of the Chicago area, was a well-respected environmentalist long before it was popular to be so.

Her visionary skills, combined with the hard work of many other dedicated volunteers as well as local publicity, helped carve the future for the IPP. The IPP became the first major rails-to-trails conversion throughout the country and is recognized nationally.

In Cook and DuPage Counties, the trail is 10-foot-wide crushed limestone. In Kane County, you will find asphalt as well as crushed limestone segments. The IPP is not a place to try to set a landspeed record. Some of the street crossings along the way are in quiet residential areas; others are in busy downtown areas. Please obey the stop signs. At most crossings, you'll find a metal post in the center of the trail as well as two posts near the sides of the path to keep out motorized vehicles. If you are biking, go slowly. Take your time and enjoy the parks, forest preserves, communities, and other points of interest along the way. A map on page 91 displays the branches and spurs of the IPP as well as the major roads.

The DuPage, Kane, and western Cook County sections, encompassing more than 52 miles of the IPP, are very well maintained and delightful places to hike or bike. Work is currently planned for 1997 to improve the remaining 3 miles of trail in Cook County.

Since this guidebook focuses on Kane and McHenry County trails, we will describe a trip on the Elgin and Aurora branches starting from their connection with the Fox River Trail. The descriptions of the Geneva and Batavia spurs describe trips back from DuPage County to the Kane County trailheads. (See Section 10 for a description of the FRT.)

Elgin Branch

The FRT coexists with the IPP for the first 2.4 miles from the trailhead in downtown Elgin north of the riverboat casino at Prairie Street as described in Section 10. In South Elgin, the two trails split with the FRT heading southwest along the river and the IPP veering first south then southeast to Wheaton. The Elgin Branch is 16.2 miles from downtown Elgin to the Wheaton trailhead at Volunteer Park.

How to get there:

The best way to get to the IPP in Kane County is on the FRT on bike or foot. However, if you have a motorized vehicle, take Route 25 or Route 31 to Kimball Street in downtown Elgin. There is a bridge crossing here if you are coming from the west. Park on the south side of Kimball in the large lot along the east bank of the river north of the casino.

From the split with the FRT in South Elgin, the IPP heads south through farmland. A trail bridge offers a safe crossing over the Chicago Central and Pacific (C. C. P.) railroad tracks. The Valley Model Railroad Association now occupies the old brick Clintonville Station that served as a substation for the electric commuter line. After another bridge crossing over busy Route 25, the trail enters DuPage County at 5.2 miles out from the trailhead in downtown Elgin. Here the path enters Pratt's Wayne Woods, a DuPage County forest preserve. You will pass through a wetland where Brewster Creek has formed a marsh to the east. A bench along the trail is a good resting spot where you can enjoy a scenic view of the marsh. On an overcast fall afternoon, I watched a great blue heron fly low over the marsh then land next to the water's edge to search for fish and frogs. This 4-foot-tall creature with long legs and long neck that curves when it flies is one of the oldest living species of birds on earth.

The trail enters a woodland area southeast of the marsh before crossing over Norton Creek. The auto road entrance into the preserve is .7 mile to the left (north) at the Powis Road crossing. There are more than 9 miles of hiking and biking trails at this preserve. Continuing on the IPP, a portable toilet and bench are at the Army Trail Road crossing. At 7.5 miles out is a steep downgrade to a railroad track crossing and a similarly steep incline east of the tracks. There are roots and stumps on the path. A side trail has been installed west of the crossing that detours around the steep downhill. Walk your bike up the hill on the east side. At busy Route 59, a long pedestrian bridge crosses this four-lane highway. Farther east a North Avenue underpass simplifies the crossing of this very busy road as well.

At 11.2 miles out, you will come to another trail intersection. The left path is the beginning of DuPage County's 12-mile Great Western Trail which runs east to Villa Park. The right path ends a short distance from the intersection. Although it rides on the same abandoned railroad right-of-way as its longer cousin, the Kane and DeKalb Counties' Great Western Trail (Section 15), there are no plans to connect these two trails. The IPP continues on the trail straight ahead. In 1996, a major regrading project greatly improved this trail crossing which previously had steep banks that required cyclists to walk their bikes up and down the embankments. As you proceed on the IPP, the trail enters a peaceful woodland in the Timber Ridge Forest Preserve.

At the County Farm/Geneva Road intersection, the IPP splits in two. The Geneva Spur heads west along the north side of Geneva Road. The Elgin Branch continues in the southeast quadrant of the intersection. More on the Geneva Spur later. Also a recently installed 1-mile trail heads north on the west side of County Farm Road to Kline Creek Farm, a living example of farm life in the 1890s. This connecting path also extends farther north to DuPage's Great Western Trail mentioned above.

Continuing on the Elgin Branch of the IPP, you will soon come to a very picturesque spot, a long straight stretch of trail shaded by a tunnel of trees. Along the trail is 130-acre Lincoln Marsh. A wooden board-walk leads to a hiking-only woodchip nature trail. Bicyclists can lock up at the bottom of the boardwalk. A bit farther south, an observation platform to the right has benches as well as stairs down to a platform by the water's edge. A second observation platform can be found left of the trail. Buffleheads, mallards, and other ducks visit the marsh in spring and fall on their way to their breeding or wintering grounds.

The trail continues southeast to Volunteer Bridge, a 160-foot-long iron truss bridge with three 70-foot spans added to cross over two city

The Illinois Prairie Path

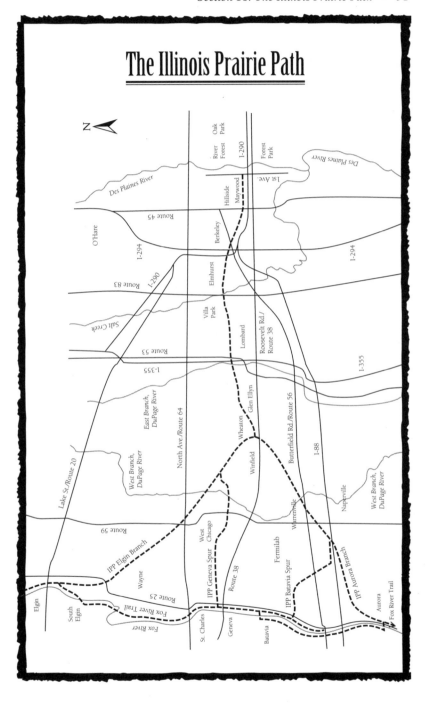

streets and a small park, as well as railroad tracks. Across the bridge is the trailhead at Volunteer Park in Wheaton. If you are starting outside of Kane County, this is the best place to park since the Elgin and Aurora Branches and the Eastern Main Stem all radiate from here.

How to get there:

Take Route 53 or I-355 from the north or south to Wheaton. From I-355, exit Roosevelt Road west for 3.3 miles to Carlton Avenue. Head north for .3 mile to the IPP trailhead in Volunteer Park at the intersection of Carlton and Liberty Drive.

You can park at the parking garage to the right for just $1 daily during the week. Weekends are free. You will also find metered parking the first block south on Carlton. Farther south is FREE four-hour parking on Carlton north of Roosevelt.

You will find a display case with information about the IPP as well as a free map and a water fountain at Volunteer Park. The name of the starting point is appropriate given the literally thousands of volunteers who have contributed their time and talents to make the IPP a premier trail system.

Geneva Spur

The newest member of the IPP family of trail branches and spurs is the path to Geneva. In 1996, the DuPage County Division of Transportation opened 3.7 miles of crushed limestone trail and designated on-road bike route from the northwest corner of the intersection of County Farm Road and Geneva Road in Winfield to Reed-Keppler Park in West Chicago. The trail runs through Winfield Mounds Forest Preserve with a bridge crossing over the West Branch of the DuPage River. Follow the bike route signs on the sidewalks and side streets of West Chicago to Reed-Keppler Park, 6.7 miles out from the Wheaton trailhead. At Reed-Keppler, the off-road trail resumes heading west to the Fox River Trail in Geneva.

The IPP crosses over seven railroad tracks leading to the Metra maintenance station just outside West Chicago. Thanks to a very long bridge built for trail users, it's an easy crossing. The path here is through mostly open prairie and marshland. Approximately 7 miles out, there are four very narrow (and easy to miss) pathways on the south side of the IPP that lead into the West Chicago Prairie Forest Preserve. The prairie trails are open to hikers only.

Farther west the IPP runs between the DuPage County Airport to the north and the Prairie Landing public golf course to the south. You'll find no trees here to provide shade nor any water fountains between Reed-Keppler Park and the Fox River in Geneva. Cornfields surround the path west of the golf course as it enters Kane County. There are only five street crossings over the 5 miles from West Chicago to Geneva. Unfortunately you'll find extremely heavy traffic and high curbs at Kirk Road. Be very careful here. I do not recommend crossing with young children. A bridge or a stoplight is definitely needed. At East Side Drive, the trail runs north (right) on a wide sidewalk to High Street. Head west for a short distance. The off-road path resumes to the right and enters Good Templar Park. The pathway crosses over a beautiful ravine on a bridge and proceeds to a switchback ramp down to Route 25. Cross Route 25 cautiously. Across the road, the Geneva Spur meets the Fox River Trail. The Geneva Spur spans 8.6 miles from Winfield to Geneva.

If you are starting out in Geneva, a good place to leave your car is Bennett Park along the Fox River north of State Street (Route 38).

How to get there:

Take Route 38/State Street to downtown Geneva. Head north on Route 25 for .3 mile to Bennett Park. Turn left (west) into the parking area along the river.

Aurora Branch

The IPP southern trailhead is in downtown Aurora at Illinois Avenue. The IPP and the FRT are contiguous from Illinois Avenue to New York Street where you will find another riverboat casino. From New York Street to Volunteer Park in Wheaton is 13.7 miles.

How to get there:

Hiking or biking on the FRT is the best way. If you have a motorized vehicle, there is a large IPP parking area east of the Fox River just north of Illinois Avenue.

At the north end of the parking area, the trail enters Gregory Park. After a hill climb, use caution at the very busy Route 25 crossing. A stoplight is definitely needed here. Follow the bike route sign east on Hankes Avenue for .1 mile. The off-road trail resumes through a residential area. The path is tree-lined for a short distance before you cross over Indian Creek. Farther east the Farnsworth Road crossing is also quite busy. Soon you will come to a major IPP improvement, the completion in 1996 of a long bridge over four-lane Eola Road. ComEd power lines run along the trail for about 1.5 miles. Soon you will come to the Elgin, Joliet, and Eastern (E. J. & E.) railroad tracks. You will want to walk your bike here. After an underpass beneath I-88, you will come to a trail intersection. The path left is the Batavia Spur which heads 5.7 miles west to the Fox River in downtown Batavia. (See below.) The Aurora Branch continues straight ahead to Wheaton. At this point, you are 6.4 miles out from the Aurora trailhead. One mile north is a single lane tunnel under Route 59. Walk your bike through the underpass. The village of Warrenville is the next milestone along the way. As you enter Warrenville, the sidewalk on the west side of Batavia Road is the beginning of the bike path which heads north into Fermilab. Here you will find a 4-mile bicycle path and 3.5 miles of hiking-only nature trails through a tallgrass prairie and adjacent woods. (See Section 17.)

East of Warrenville, an IPP bridge crosses over the West Branch of the DuPage River. This is a peaceful woodsy area through the Warrenville Grove Forest Preserve. A tunnel under Butterfield Road leads past a large horse farm. The serene trail is lined with trees. At the Wiesbrook Road crossing, the IPP continues straight ahead. An interesting side trip is Herrick Lake and Danada Forest Preserves with 9.4 miles of crushed limestone multi-use trail. To visit these preserves take the sidewalk on the west side of Wiesbrook .5 mile south to the intersection with Butterfield Road. Diagonally across the street is a trail entrance to Herrick Lake Forest Preserve. Back on the IPP heading north to Wheaton, be careful crossing Orchard Road, a busy street where cars come fast around a curve in the road. The off-road trail ends south of Roosevelt Road. Take the limestone path north of

Roosevelt along Carlton Avenue to the trailhead at Volunteer Park in Wheaton.

Batavia Spur

There are practically no trees here, mostly a lot of farmland. If you need a break, there's a bench where you can sit and listen to the corn grow. Soon you will come to another railroad track crossing. Farther west you will find a new underpass at Eola Road. Completed as part of a road widening project in 1996, this is another major improvement on the IPP. Two miles from the start of the spur, the pathway is again tree-lined and passes by two ponds. At 9.8 miles out from the Wheaton trailhead, the path enters Kane County. In spring, blooming white and pink honeysuckle shrubs and wildflowers border the trail. At 11.2 miles out from the Wheaton trailhead, the path crosses very busy Kirk Road just west of Fermilab. I finally got across after a long wait. I don't recommend crossing with small children until the overpass planned for 1997 is completed. If you take the asphalt path on the west side of Kirk Road heading north for .8 mile, you can access the Fermilab bike path (mentioned above) at Pine Street.

West of Fermilab, the Kane County trail is asphalt-surfaced and tree-lined. After crossing Raddant and Hart Roads, you will come to the intersection with the Fox River Trail at 13.5 miles out from the start in Wheaton. One mile farther south on the FRT is the Red Oak Nature Center (Section18). The Batavia Spur continues north for another 1.1 miles contiguous with the FRT. The western trailhead is at the foot of the stairs leading up to Wilson Street in downtown Batavia.

How to get there:

If you are starting out from Batavia, you'll find plenty of free parking in the downtown area near the trailhead. Glenwood Park Forest Preserve on Route 25 south of Batavia is another good spot.

Main Stem (Eastern Branch)

The eastern Main Stem section consists of 15 miles of trail from downtown Wheaton to First Avenue in Maywood. Assuming you parked near the Wheaton trailhead at Volunteer Park as described

The Illinois Prairie Path

Running on the Illinois Prairie Path

above, head east on the wide sidewalk on the north side of Liberty Drive to West Street. The off-road trail starts at West Street near the Wheaton Metra station. As you pass through Founder's Park, observe the rock monument with the inscription " 'Footpaths are defended with spirit by their users.' May Theilgaard Watts."

After several street crossings, the surrounding environment quickly changes from the downtown business area to a quieter residential neighborhood (1.4 miles out from the Wheaton trailhead). Honeysuckle bushes and trees on both sides of the trail provide a peaceful shady passage. On your right 1.8 miles out is Hoffman Park with picnic tables, playground equipment, ball fields, and a water fountain.

After 2.9 miles, you will cross Main Street in Glen Ellyn and proceed through the Metra train station area. Prairie Path Park in downtown Glen Ellyn has benches, a water fountain, and a bike rack. East of downtown watch out for a fairly steep hill on both sides of the Taylor Avenue crossing. Here you will pass a small prairie restoration area planted in 1975 by Glenbard West High School students. A bridge crosses over the East Branch of the DuPage River at 4.6 miles. Twice swept away by the 100-year floods of 1972, then later burned by vandals, the bridge is a testimonial to the persistence and dedication of the volunteers and professionals who maintain the IPP.

At 4.6 miles out, you will pass over I-355 and Route 53 on a huge bridge built for IPP users. The community of Lombard follows with another main street crossing at 5.4 miles out. As you leave the downtown area, the mature trees provide welcome shade. At 7 miles out, you will enter Villa Park. Streetlights line the path through a long linear park. Playgrounds, a water fountain, and picnic tables are available. At 8 miles, you will pass the Villa Park Historical Society Museum. Housed in the former train station for the long departed electric line, the museum displays memorabilia from the defunct railroad and the Wander Corporation (maker of Ovaltine). Hours are Tuesday–Friday 2–6 p.m. and Saturday–Sunday 10 a.m. to 4 p.m. A bike rack, water fountain, and restroom are available. History buffs will enjoy stopping for a visit. Two short blocks north of the museum on Villa Avenue is the eastern trailhead for the Great Western Trail.

At 8.3 miles out, you will enter the city of Elmhurst. Two bridge crossings take the trail user over first Route 83 and then Salt Creek. There are plans to develop an extensive 38-mile Salt Creek Greenway Trail extending north to the Ned Brown Forest Preserve in Cook County and southeast to the 20-mile Centennial Trail currently under development. (See Section 22 for more information.)

In Elmhurst, community park district volunteers have restored 6 acres of tallgrass prairie from Salt Creek to Spring Road along the IPP. At the Berkeley Street intersection, you will discover an interpretive garden labeling the native prairie plants our ancestors discovered hundreds of years ago. Blooming in mid-summer are purple coneflowers with their large lavender drooping petals. You will also find the lavender-hued blazing star which blooms in an unusual manner, from the top down. The more careful observer might discover a less common prairie species, the rattlesnake master. This plant has tight, round spiny balls upon which miniature white flowers bloom.

Many trees incompatible with the prairie environment were removed from this area. While I love wooded trails, I have also come to appreciate and enjoy the diversity of plant and animal life and the subtle changing colors found in a prairie. As you hike or bike your way through the IPP communities, you will find several prairie restoration projects. The Elmhurst Great Western and the West Chicago Prairie are the largest.

Water fountains and picnic tables are available at Wild Meadows Trace Park at Spring Avenue 9 miles out and also farther east.

Leaving Elmhurst (at 10.6 miles), the IPP runs under I-294 entering Cook County. The path under the bridge is bumpy. The trail continues through the Cook County community of Berkeley. A park with picnic tables, drinking water, restrooms, and a bike rack is east of the bridge. The IPP temporarily ends in Hillside shortly after a bridge over Wolf Road at 11.5 miles out. I suggest turning around at the small electric substation on the trail. Farther east are 2.5 miles of path and an on-road detour from Butterfield Road in Hillside to Mannheim Road in Bellwood. From Mannheim Road to First Avenue in Maywood, the trail surface is rough in spots due to water main repair. Also, there were obstructions on the path when I visited. The Illinois Department of Natural Resources plans to improve the Cook County section in 1997. Cook County agencies plan to extend the path .5 mile east across the Des Plaines River to the Chicago Transit Authority station at Des Plaines Avenue in Forest Park. From there, a multi-use trail is planned to head south along the river to Summit as part of the Grand Illinois Trail. (See Section 23.)

If you are interested in becoming a member of The Illinois Prairie Path organization, you can obtain a membership application by writing to The Illinois Prairie Path, P. O. Box 1086, Wheaton, IL 60189, or calling 630-752-0120. Members receive a quarterly newsletter and a large IPP map. Your contribution will help maintain and improve the IPP.

The Cook County section is maintained by the Illinois Department of Natural Resources. The DuPage County portion is maintained by the DuPage County Division of Transportation. For further information, call 630-682-7318. In Kane County, the Kane County Forest Preserve District maintains the spurs and the Elgin Branch. The telephone number is 630-232-5980. The Aurora Branch is maintained by the Fox Valley Park District, 630-897-0516.

Northern Kane County Forest Preserve Trails

Three forest preserves in rural areas of northern Kane County offer quiet, secluded spots for hiking. The pathways are mostly mowed turf or packed earth-surfaced trails.

Binnie Forest Preserve

West of Carpentersville and north of I-90 is a 127-acre forest preserve with unmarked trails through open fields and woods.

How to get there:

Take Route 72 west of Spring Hill Mall and Sleepy Hollow to Randall Road. Turn right on Randall. Proceed north to Binnie Road. Go west .9 mile past the golf course to the forest preserve entrance on the north side of the road.

North of the parking area is a mowed turf pathway that leads to overlapping .8- and 1.5-mile loop trails. Pine trees line the trail in spots.

Rutland Forest Preserve

A peaceful place west of the village of Gilberts and south of I-90 has a short trail through tall oak trees. Eakin Creek runs through the east side of the preserve.

How to get there:

From Route 31 in Elgin, take Big Timber Road 3.1 miles west past Randall Road and Route 72. The preserve entrance is north.

An auto road loops through this secluded 58-acre preserve. You will find a small parking area in an oak grove along the road. A mile or so of unmarked woodchip and packed earth-surfaced path criss-crosses through the hilly woodland inside the auto road loop. You will also find some mowed turf equestrian trails on the preserve's periphery. On a breezy late October day, I hiked through an oak savanna next to a marsh filled with cattails as well as a large flock of red-winged black-birds screeching in unison. The auto road is a good place for a short hike or bike ride.

Hampshire Forest Preserve

The 8 miles of trail here are primarily used by equestrians, but are also open for hiking. Mostly mowed turf trails run through open fields, a large woodland, and nearby wetlands.

How to get there:

Take Route 20 in northwestern Kane County past the junction of Routes 20, 47, and 72 to Allen Road. Turn right. You will find the preserve entrance .6 mile northwest of Route 20 on the right side of Allen Road.

Similar to Rutland, an .8-mile auto road loops through the preserve. The woodland area is primarily inside the loop surrounded by open fields and wetlands. The mowed turf trails are mostly on the edge of this 217-acre preserve with a short trail through the woods inside the auto road loop.

You will find picnic tables, shelters, water pumps, and restrooms at all three sites described above. These preserves are open for cross-country skiing and Rutland is also open for snowmobiling.

Burnidge Forest Preserve

Kane County's largest preserve has 9 miles of hiking trails through 486 acres of rolling hills and prairies as well as vehicular and tent camping sites. You will enjoy 2 miles of hiking-only trails meandering through oak woods as well as 7 miles of trails open for equestrians and hikers.

With volunteer help, the Kane County Forest Preserve District is restoring the prairie and woods through burns, seed collecting, brush clearing, and seedling plantings. By these methods, the latent seed bank beneath the ground can be released. What will result is a much more diverse and healthy ecosystem. Already forest preserve officials and volunteers have found some unique plant communities here as a result of burns. Bog arrow grass and rattlesnake plantain are just some of the plants reclaiming the natural areas of Burnidge.

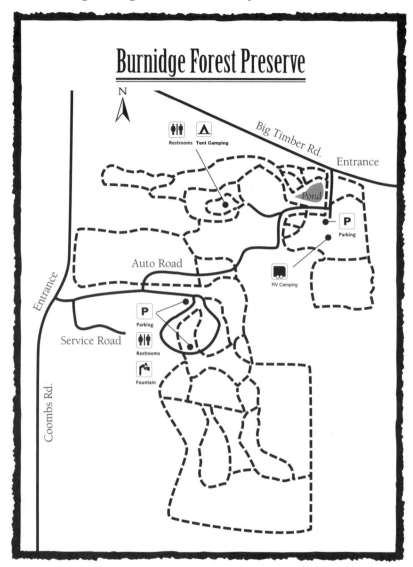

Burnidge Forest Preserve

N

Big Timber Rd.

Entrance

Restrooms Tent Camping

Pond

P
Parking

Auto Road

RV Camping

Entrance

P
Parking

Service Road

Restrooms

Fountain

Coombs Rd.

How to get there:

From Randall Road on the northwest side of Elgin (north of Route 20 and south of I-90) take Big Timber Road west for 1.4 miles. The Paul Wolff campground entrance is south of the road. To park closer to the wooded hiking trails continue west on Big Timber another .8

mile to Coombs Road. Turn left and proceed south .7 mile. Take
another left into Burnidge Forest Preserve. The parking area to the
right is the trailhead for mowed turf paths heading north and south.

A .6-mile auto road loops around a woodland south of the parking
area. Take the path inside the auto road loop heading south. Filled with
beautiful ridges and ravines, the trails winding through the mature oak
forest are quite hilly. Numerous trail intersections make it easy to get
lost. Bring a compass.

South of the forest, a trail heads through open fields to the preserve
border along the Metra railroad tracks. Here the terrain is less hilly.
Hundreds of tall pines surround the path as you head back north.

North of the Coombs Road parking area, a mowed turf equestrian
trail heads to the primitive (tent) camping area. Here a path winds
through a woodland to individual camping sites with picnic tables and
fire rings. A small creek runs along the campground.

A water pump, picnic tables, and restrooms are available at the
Coombs Road entrance. There is a public phone at the campground
entrance. An auto road connects the campground to the Burnidge

Jerry Hennen

Cross-country skier at Burnidge Forest Preserve

Forest Preserve. Tent camping is available on weekends in spring, summer, and fall. RV camping is available year-round. Reservations are not required. Call the Kane County Forest Preserve District at 630-695-8410 for more information. All the trails are open for cross-country skiing in winter.

Tekakwitha Woods Nature Center

On my first visit to this serene place, great white trillium blanketed the hills of a beautiful oak/hickory forest on the high banks of the Fox River.

How to get there:

Ride your bike on the Fox River Trail if you can. The trail goes right by the nature center entrance. (See Section 10.) If you must use a motorized vehicle, take Route 25 south of Route 20 in Elgin and north of Route 64 in St. Charles to May Lane. Follow the nature center signs west on May Lane to Weber Drive. Head north on Weber to the nature center parking area at Villa Marie Road. (See map.)

The trails here are for hiking only. You'll find a bike rack near the nature center. Follow the asphalt pathway down the hill past the nature center building to a woodchip foot path that winds its way down to and along the river banks. There are 1.3 miles of trail here through the forest and open grasslands where prairie and savanna areas are being restored. During my early May visit Danielle and Valerie, naturalists at the nature center, showed me the unusual yellow

Tekakwitha Woods Nature Center

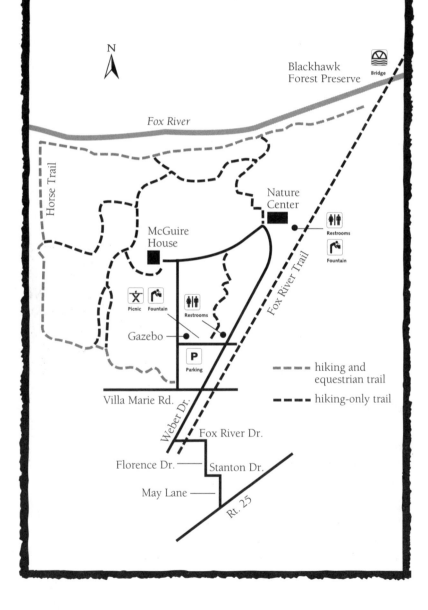

violets, the lovely spring beauties, dutchman's-breeches, and the great white trillium. This tri-petaled white wildflower appears like snow in spring. The blooms only last for a short time and fade to pink as spring progresses. In the nature center, you'll find displays and exhibits, children's activities, and a nature library. Come in October to

Scouts at Tekakwitha Nature Center

enjoy the beautiful fall colors.

Programs and activities are offered year-round. Call 847-741-8350 for nature center hours and more information. The trails are open for cross-country skiing in winter.

Great Western Trail

An abandoned Great Western railroad line has a new life as a 17.4-mile greenway trail from St. Charles to Sycamore in DeKalb County. This pathway is one of the most rural in Chicagoland passing through wide open spaces comprised mostly of farmland with huge cornfields. Ribbons of prairies and small woodlands border the trail.

How to get there:

Take Route 64 west of downtown St. Charles to Randall Road. Head north for .4 mile to Dean Road. Head west for .3 mile to the Great Western trailhead parking area on the south side of the road.

You will find a water pump, picnic tables, a shelter, a grill, and restroom at the trailhead. Be sure to stock up on water. Refreshments are available in three small villages along the way; but not directly adjacent to the trail. The trailhead is in the southern portion of LeRoy Oakes Forest Preserve. Across Dean Road is the entrance to the main part of the preserve. Here you will find a hiking trail as well as a pioneer school and a brick farmhouse built in 1843. (See Section 16.)

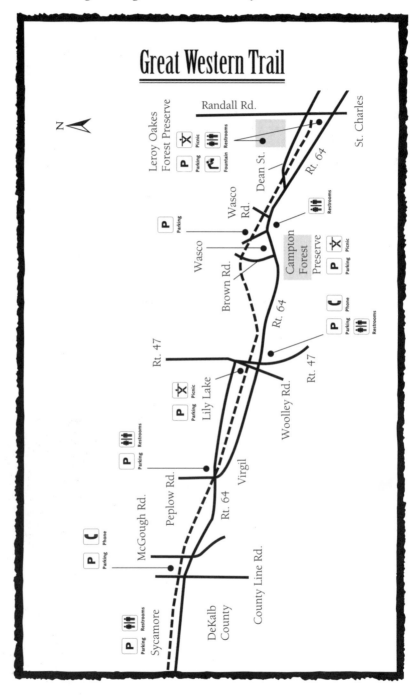

The Great Western Trail, like many former railways, is flat and straight. The only hills and curves come at the start through the forest preserve. The trail surface is asphalt at the beginning and a few other areas along the way that are prone to washouts. Most of the trail is a well-maintained crushed gravel and limestone surface. As you start out, note the 3-acre Horlock Hill Prairie left of the trail. In the 1970s, Robert R. Horlock, and his biology class at St. Charles High School replanted native prairie grasses and forbs here. Each student cared for his or her own plot. A short woodchip trail to the south leads to a wooden platform viewing area overlooking the prairie. The trail heads downhill and soon enters a beautiful woodland. Here the surface changes to crushed gravel. The elevated roadbed forms a ridge running through the woods with embankments as tall as 20-feet-high on either side. So stay on the trail! The pathway is compact and drains well. I noticed little bumpiness from the horses who share the trail. The first road crossing is at Dean Road about 1.6 mile out. Easily visible mile markers along the way help gauge your progress.

Farther west, large bridges at Hidden Oaks Drive and Burlington Road make for safe passage. Watch out for the motorized vehicle barricade in the middle of the trail as you cross the bridges. Route 64 parallels the trail here and for most of the rest of the way out to Sycamore. Note the small red signs along the trail. Designations such as "DCFPD 38 W 000" identify the location for emergency personnel.

The first village you'll encounter at 3.2 miles out is Wasco. Food and drink is available to the south. Here the trail is less shaded. Prairie grasses and new growth trees line the path. In spring and summer, you will probably share the trail with muskrat, rabbits, chipmunks, and red-winged blackbirds as I did. Most quickly dart into the protective foliage. But one young muskrat thought he could outrun my bike down the trail. Suddenly he stopped, turned, and looked at me standing his ground. A last second swerve avoided a collision and he darted into the ground cover. Several creeks and marsh areas along the way offer an opportunity to see great blue herons and other wading birds.

As you head west, cornfields and farmhouses replace the large new homes found farther east on the outskirts of St. Charles. Agri-vistas

Kane County Forest Preserve District

Peck Road Bridge on the Great Western Trail

offer views of corn, farmhouses, and a lot of sky. I encountered some large loose gravel at farm road intersections along the way. At 7.9 miles out, a nearby highway sign informs the trail user that Sycamore is 11 miles and Oregon is 45 miles. And I did not even notice Colorado! Although a light dusting of cottonwood seeds did give a wintry look to the warm May day.

You will soon pass by Lilly Lake at Route 47. The lake from whence the village got its name is long gone having been drained in the 1930s to make way for a paved auto road.

At 10.8 miles out, you will come to the village of Virgil and Norm's Cold Pop sign near the trail across Route 64. A bit farther is the Sycamore Speedway and at 14.2 miles out, DeKalb County at County Line Road. DeKalb County and Kane County Forest Preserve District personnel are restoring and expanding the native prairie along the trail. Colorful forbs and prairie grasses grow along the trail near Larson and Lovell Roads in DeKalb County. Also you'll find a small rest area at Larson Road. Soon you will see a large blue water tower in the distance serving notice that the trail's end is near.

The western trailhead is 17.4 miles out at Route 64 and the eastern outskirts of Sycamore, the county seat of DeKalb County. There is parking and a picnic table available here. Take Airport Road .2 mile south of the trail to Sycamore Community Park to find water, restrooms, shelters, and picnic areas. Use caution crossing Route 64. You will need to continue another mile into downtown Sycamore or head back to Virgil for other forms of sustenance.

The Great Western Trail is open dawn to dusk. The eastern section near St. Charles has much more traffic on the trail than the western section. On a sunny weekday in mid-May I biked about 8 miles on the west side without passing a soul. Picnic tables or benches at some road intersections offer an opportunity to rest. The Great Western is open to cross-country skiers.

Work is underway to construct an off-road connection between the Fox River Trail and the Great Western in 1997 or 1998 via the existing River Bend Bike Path and a new trail along Randall Road. Also there are plans to extend the Great Western southwest to the town of DeKalb.

For more information, call the Kane County Forest Preserve District at 630-232-5980 or the DeKalb County Forest Preserve District on 815-895-7191.

Central Kane County Forest Preserve Trails

Two forest preserves west of St. Charles offer rustic hiking trails amid all the new home developments.

LeRoy Oakes Forest Preserve

Across the street from the trailhead for the Great Western Trail (Section 15), you will find a 1-mile hiking trail along Ferson Creek in this 264-acre preserve.

How to get there:

Take Route 64 west of St. Charles to Randall Road. Head north 1 mile to Dean Street. Turn left (west) and proceed .5 mile to the preserve entrance on the north side of the street. Drive past the historic Durant-Peterson House and the Pioneer Sholes School and proceed to the parking area at the end of the auto road.

A packed earth trail runs for about a mile through a peaceful woodland and along the bank of Ferson Creek north and east of the parking area. Watch your footing on the scenic 40-foot-high bluff overlooking the creek. You will find picnic tables, a water pump, and restrooms near the parking area, and benches along the creek.

Both historical buildings are open to visitors on Sunday afternoons in summer and fall. The Durant-Peterson House was built in 1843. Today it serves as a living history museum depicting what life was like here 150 years ago. Nearby is a restored one-room schoolhouse. Call 630-377-6424 for more information.

Campton Forest Preserve

Southwest of the village of Wasco is a 305-acre forest preserve. Mill Creek runs through the preserve's east side. Wetlands surround the creek. Rolling hills and woodlands comprise much of the western part of the preserve.

How to get there:

Take Route 64 west of St. Charles through the village of Wasco to Town Hall Road. Turn left. The preserve entrance is on your left.

A 4-mile mowed turf and packed earth trail winds its way through

Kane County Forest Preserve District

Ferson Creek at LeRoy Oakes Forest Preserve

the rolling hills. Near the parking area, a commanding and scenic view of the valley to the east greets you. Follow the mowed turf trail down the hill. Markers point out the hiking path some of which is closed to equestrians. Hiking through the oak woodland, you'll encounter a very steep decline on the trail down into the valley. A waterpump, shelter, picnic tables, and restrooms are available next to the parking area.

Trails at both sites are open for cross-country skiing in winter.

Fermilab Bike Path and Nature Trails

Two hundred years ago, buffalo roamed tallgrass prairie stretching across what is now DuPage and Kane Counties. Potowatami hunters came south from their villages along the river. Their arrows flew straight and found their mark. This land is presently occupied by the Fermi National Accelerator Laboratory in Batavia. Operated by a consortium of U.S., Canadian, Italian, and Japanese Universities, for the U. S. Department of Energy, Fermilab is home to thousands of scientists from many countries. They focus on high-energy physics—the study of understanding the ultimate building blocks of nature. To help carry out their mission, they built the Tevatron, the "highest energy particle accelerator on earth," buried in a 4-mile circumference tunnel. The U. S. Department of Energy acquired cornfields, wetlands, and forest to build the accelerator and required facilities. In 1974, The Nature Conservancy and some local volunteers began reconstructing a tallgrass prairie on 600 acres inside the Tevatron's 4-mile ring. Most of the original prairie had been plowed under by early settlers and farmers to grow corn and other crops. Today more than 1,000 acres of tallgrass prairie thrive across the Fermilab site. Additional plantings are anticipated. Controlled burns help maintain the vibrancy of the prairie grasses and wildflowers. You can also wander through or near upland forest, floodplain woods, oak savannas, pastures, croplands, lakes, streams, and wetlands. Because of this diverse habitat, more than 250 species of birds have been seen at Fermilab including 80 that breed there regularly. Fermilab is a preferred site for geese, shorebirds, owls, shrikes, and grassland birds.

A 3.6-mile bike path runs through the grounds along Batavia Road. Two prairie trails, .5 mile and 1.2 miles long, lead through part of the reconstructed prairie. The prairie trail connects with 1.8 miles of pathways through a woods to the east.

How to get there:

By auto, take Kirk Road .8 mile north of Butterfield Road to the west entrance or from Route 59 take Batavia Road west to the east entrance. The west entrance is open from 6 a.m. to 8 p.m. seven days a week. The east entrance is open for public use from 6:30–8 p.m. only on Monday through Friday and 6 a.m. to 8 p.m. on Saturday and Sunday. You can also travel to Fermilab on bike or on foot from the Illinois Prairie Path (IPP). From the Aurora Branch, take the concrete sidewalk/bike path west along Batavia Road starting at the intersection with Butterfield Road in Warrenville 1.9 miles to the east entrance. If you are traveling from the west, take the IPP Batavia Spur to Kirk Road. Head north .8 mile on the asphalt bike path on the west side of Kirk Road. Enter Fermilab at the stoplight at Pine Road.

When you hike or bike through Fermilab, stop at Wilson Hall. You can chain your bike to the railings on either side of the entrance. A giant pendulum, various displays, an information desk, cafeteria, restrooms, and drinking water can be found on the first floor. Take a visitor elevator to the 15th floor to view a video as well as exhibits about the work done at Fermilab. You will also find an extensive display of arrowheads and other artifacts from the Native Americans that hunted here. Before Fermilab was constructed, August J. Mier, an

Fermilab Visual Media Services

Herd of buffalo near Wilson Hall

amateur archaeologist, searched for arrowheads and other Native American implements. He learned by the type of arrowheads found that this land served as a hunting ground for thousands of years. From the panoramic view of the 15th floor windows, you can see the tallgrass prairie, the nature trails and bike path, and the main ring in which the accelerator is housed. On a clear day, the Chicago skyline is visible to the northeast. You can also see something found nowhere else in the Chicago area—a herd of approximately 75 buffalo residing in a pasture northeast of Wilson Hall, a reminder that their ancestors freely wandered here.

The bike path runs 3.6 miles from the east to the west entrance. Along the way, you'll pass two lakes, the Fermilab Village, buffalo grazing in a pasture, Wilson Hall, marsh, woodlands, and the trail-head for the nature trails through the prairie. Most of the bike path is off-road asphalt surfaced, but a section west of Wilson Hall is on-road with a white line separating the bike route from auto traffic.

From Wilson Hall, follow the bike path signs north on Pine Street, a one-way road heading to the west entrance. Here you'll find the

Fermilab Bike Path and Nature Trails

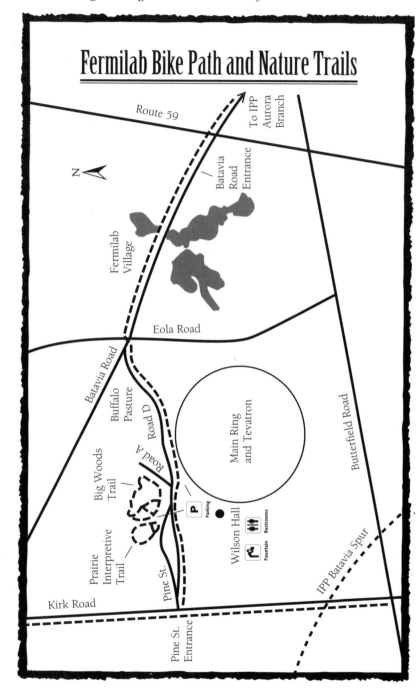

prairie trails. In June of 1986, a 50-acre tract was planted with prairie grass seeds. Today Indian grass and big bluestem flourish. A .5-mile woodchip interpretive trail loops through the prairie. You'll find signs along the way describing the ecosystem and restoration process. Two hundred species of wildflowers inhabit the prairie. Many of these plants are solely dependent on specific insects which pollinate them. The thousands of insects including butterflies and moths which live here are part of a complex web. In late summer and early fall, you can stand in 7-foot-tall big bluestem and listen to the buzzing sound of insects hidden within the grasses' confines. Big bluestem is nicknamed turkey foot grass because of its stiff turkey foot-like branches.

From the interpretive trail, a 1.2-mile outer loop takes the hiker farther into the prairie. Wandering through this area gave me a sense of what settlers coming to America several centuries ago encountered when they first set foot in this new land.

East of the prairie trail is a 1.8-mile packed earth pathway that loops through a large woods. You can enter the woods from the interpretive trail. The prairie nature trails are open for hiking only. The bike path and forest trails are open for cross-country skiing in the winter.

Call 630-840-3351 for more information.

Red Oak Nature Center

Along the east bank of the Fox River, south of Batavia, is a nature center nestled in a 40-acre oak and maple forest.

How to get there:

By auto take Route 25 three miles south of Batavia and .5 mile north of Route 56 in North Aurora. The parking area is on the west side of Route 25. The best way to get there is on bike on the Fox River Trail (FRT)! You can lock your bike at one of several racks near the entrance or in front of the nature center building.

You'll find four short hiking trails at Red Oak. The .5-mile Dolomite Trail and the .3-mile Turtle Trail wind through the woodlands around the center. A seasonal interpretive booklet is available at the nature center explaining points of interest along the Dolomite Trail.

Directly behind the nature center, you will find a large observation deck along the Turtle Trail extending out over the river. This is a good place to sit and watch the river flow by and to enjoy the

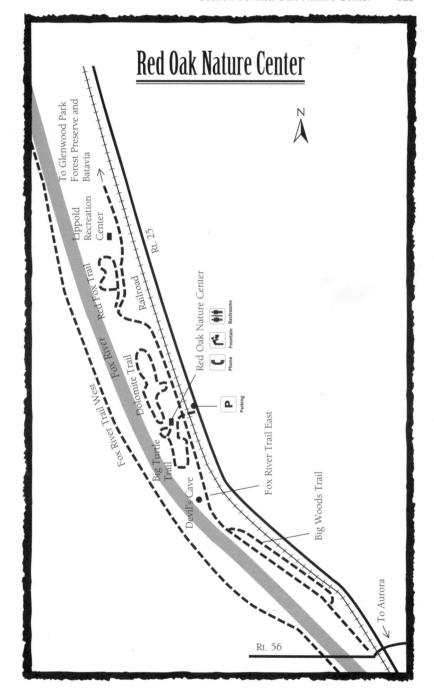

Red Oak Nature Center

N

To Glenwood Park
Forest Preserve and
Batavia

Lippold
Recreation
Center

Rt. 25

Red Fox Trail

Railroad

Fox River

Red Oak Nature Center

Restrooms

Fountain

Phone

Dolomite Trail

P
Parking

Fox River Trail West

Big Turtle
Trail

Devil's Cave

Fox River Trail East

Big Woods Trail

To Aurora

Rt. 56

Kane County Forest Preserve District

Devil's Cave at Red Oak Nature Center

red oaks identified by the pointed ends of the leaves.

Early settlers found an old Native American trail here; today we can walk the same ground enjoying nearby Big Turtle River, named by the Potowatamis who found many snapping turtles and other species along the Fox. The Red Fox Trail lies north of the nature center. Take the FRT .5 mile north to a mowed grass area on the left. At the time of writing, there was no sign on the FRT. Head downhill through the grassy area. A sign to the right identifies the trailhead. Constructed by Eagle Scouts, this .4-mile loop trail is a bit more rugged than those around the nature center. The pathway has some tree stumps, roots, and stones. On your way back to the nature center, you will pass a picnic area with grills.

South of the nature center are two more areas of interest along the FRT. Watch for the cave sign painted in yellow on the asphalt trail. Take the stairs down to a small cave in a dolomite rock outcropping. There is a tragic legend from early settler days on how Devil's Cave got its name; details are available at the nature center. A short distance south of Devil's Cave is the start of the 1.5-mile Big Woods Trail. On the east side of the FRT, a narrow footpath heads into the woodlands. The path meanders up and down the wooded river bank parallel with the river. The trail ends at the FRT near water's edge. Here the path is less than ten feet from the river.

Maps and other information as well as water and restrooms are available inside the nature center. The six-foot-wide trails near the nature center are open for cross-country skiing in winter. The Fox Valley Park District offers programs year-round at the nature center. Hours are 9 a.m. to 4 p.m. weekdays and 10 a.m. to 3 p.m. weekends. Call 630-897-1808 for more information.

Southern Kane County Forest Preserve Trails

Near Batavia and Aurora, you will find two forest preserves with trails through or along wetlands.

Nelson Lake Marsh

For generations, we have drained wetlands to make way for farms, homes, offices, and factories. These wetlands were seen as wastelands, swamps, areas that had nothing to offer. Today we know differently. Wetlands are nature's sponges, soaking up pollution before it can get into our streams, rivers, and lakes and even into our drinking water. A marsh is nature's storm water retention pond, preventing flooding by slowing the flow of rainwater. Today, Nelson Lake Marsh, owned by the Kane County Forest Preserve District, is valued. Indeed it is a designated Illinois Nature Preserve, protected from future development. This 10,000-year-old wonder attracts a host of reptiles, amphibians, plants, insects, mammals, and birds. Some 162 plant species including the bog willow, dwarf birch, and marsh marigold thrive here. Some 120 bird species have been observed here from March through September including at least 11 that are state-endangered or state-threatened. Migratory birds such as snow geese and wood ducks use the lake in spring. Come summer, king rails, threatened in Illinois, nest in the wetland reeds. The ponds attract bellowing bullfrogs and painted turtles in summer. And butterflies abound feasting on wildflower nectar. From May through August you have the chance of observing monarchs, viceroys, alfalfas, skipperlings, swallowtails, and other unusual lepidopteral species. Enjoy!

How to get there:

Head west from Batavia on Main Street, 1.5 miles past Randall Road to Nelson Lake Road. Go south to the pull off parking area on the right.

Attempts to drain the marsh for farmland in the early 1900s were unsuccessful due to numerous natural springs. Ponds near the lake were formed by peat mining operations. Today you can hike along the edge of the marsh, lake, and ponds and through the adjacent woodland. Stay on the 6-foot-wide mowed turf or woodchip trails to protect the natural areas. Approximately 1.5 miles of hiking-only trail wanders through the 300-acre preserve.

In the summer, come prepared for mosquitoes and pesky horseflies.

Oakhurst Forest Preserve

A large lake, marshland, and scenic view from atop a large hill can be

A beaver lodge at Nelson Lake Marsh

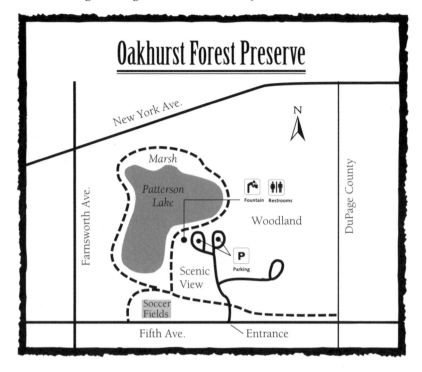

found at 331-acre Oakhurst Forest Preserve east of Aurora. One and eight-tenth miles of asphalt and crushed limestone trails run around the lake and adjoining wetland, through a forest, and along 5th Avenue. The pathways are open for biking as well as hiking.

How to get there:

Take Farnsworth Avenue .7 mile south of New York Street in Aurora to 5th Avenue. Head east (left) .6 mile past the soccer fields to the preserve's main entrance on the left side.

Excavation for 55-acre Patterson Lake in 1983 left a very large mound of dirt which today is the highest elevation in the area. Climb the hill near the boat launch parking area to get a scenic view of the lake and surrounding woodlands. Oakhurst is a favorite spot for bird watchers; the wetlands attract many different species. Water, shelters, picnic tables, and restrooms can be found near the lake.

The trails at both sites are open for cross-country skiing in winter.

Virgil L. Gilman Nature Trail

The Fox Valley Park District and the Kane County Forest Preserve District have worked together to convert two abandoned railroad right-of-ways into a shady 14.3-mile trail from Business Route 30 southeast of Aurora through Bliss Woods Forest Preserve north of Sugar Grove and on to Waubonsee Community College. The eastern section crosses Waubonsee Creek and the Fox River as it runs through residential neighborhoods on the south side of Aurora. The western section is more sylvan through woodlands along Blackberry Creek.

At the time of writing, work was underway on a 3-mile addition, which extends the trail westward from Bliss Woods on a new bridge over Blackberry Creek to Waubonsee Community College along Route 47. The western trailhead is in a parking area south of the campus near an oak grove.

How to get there:

To reach the trailhead in Bliss Woods take Route 47 south of I-88 and north of Sugar Grove. Head east on Bliss Road .4 mile to the forest preserve. Take

Near the trailhead in Bliss Woods Forest Preserve

the first entrance into the preserve. Follow the auto road under the overhanging branches of huge oak trees to the right to park near the trail.

The eastern trailhead is southeast of Aurora on Hill Avenue just across the Kendall County border .3 mile north of the Route 30/Route 34 intersection. Look for a small sign at the trailhead that's not very visible from the road. The best indicator is the large white inflated sports dome south of the trailhead. You'll find numerous parking areas along the trail several of which are shown on the map.

On my first visit, I parked at beautiful 280-acre Bliss Woods, a popular camping site. Here the early settlers celebrated their first July 4th under an elm tree in 1834. From the parking area farthest north, take the gravel pathway into the woods. You will quickly come to a trail intersection. The path left heads northwest 3 miles to Waubonsee Community College. The path right heads southeast to Aurora. The trail to Aurora is mostly a quiet, shady trek through woodlands and along Blackberry Creek. After a few small hills and curves in the forest preserve, the path is relatively flat and straight. The trail surface is

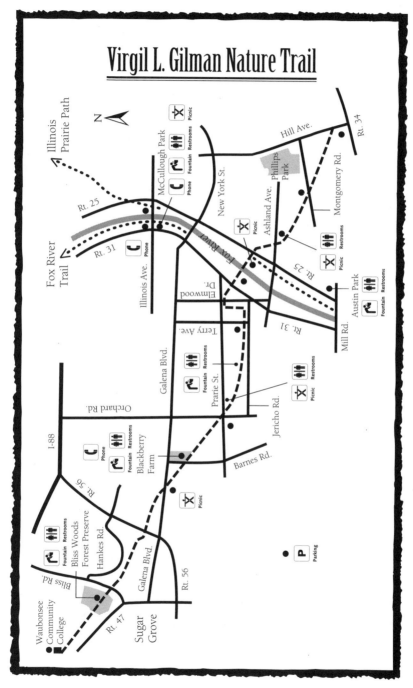

asphalt east of the preserve and then crushed limestone through the lowland areas along the creek. I first visited shortly after the deluge of July 1996, when almost 17 inches of rain fell on Aurora over one 24-hour period. Normally placid Blackberry Creek became a raging torrent and swept away many large trees that lay in its path. A significant portion of the trail was washed away, which was quickly repaired by forest preserve district and park district personnel. Two miles out from Bliss Woods is a trail underpass at busy four-lane Route 56. During the rainy season the underpass is often flooded. A side trail leads up to Route 56 for a road crossing. However, I do not recommend crossing with young children or inexperienced bicyclists. (Hopefully the underpass will be dry on all your visits.)

At the Galena Boulevard crossing 3 miles out is a picnic table and trail parking area. After you cross the road, note the sundial and stone wall with imbedded seating areas. This is the first of eight such structures built many years ago to prevent motorized vehicles from entering the trail at road crossings. Go slowly on the path around the stone walls to avoid a close encounter with another trail user. The next street crossing at Barnes Road leads to the Blackberry Historical Farm-Village a short distance to the north. Blackberry offers children's rides, museums, a pioneer cabin, farm animals, early American crafts and special events. Also an aquatic center is planned for completion in 1998.

At the Prairie Street/Orchard Avenue intersection 4.7 miles out, use the pedestrian buttons for a safe crossing. The trail continues in the southeast quadrant of the intersection where you will find a water fountain and shelter. At 6.8 miles out, the off-road trail ends. The next mile runs on the streets through a mixed residential/industrial area. If 13.5 miles round-trip is enough, head back to Bliss Woods. If you want to see the Fox River and other sights on the remaining 6 miles of trail, head left (north) on Terry Avenue for .1 mile to Rathbone Avenue. Watch carefully for the trail route markers along the streets. The streets had a lot of pot holes and loose rocks on my visit. Take Rathbone for .3 mile to Elmwood Drive. Head left (north) for .2 mile to Ridgeway Avenue. Turn right, proceed .3 mile, and cross the railroad tracks. The off-road trail picks up again on the east side of a trail parking area as you enter Copley Park. The Fox Valley Park District had to completely rebuild a trail section east of Copley Park as a result of the 1996 flood.

After passing Lake Street/Route 31, you will come to a truss bridge over the Fox River. On one of my visits, a great white egret stood near the water's edge looking for its next meal. On the east bank at 8.3 miles out is a parking area in South Broadway Park as well as a connection to the newest section of the Fox River Trail which heads south along the river 1.2 miles to Mill Street in Montgomery. Construction is planned for an extension of the Fox River Trail north to New York Street. This will connect the Virgil Gilman with the existing Fox River Trail. (See section 10 for more information about the Fox River Trail.)

To continue southeast on the Virgil Gilman Trail, cross Broadway/Route 25 and Lincoln Avenues. Here the trail runs through residential neighborhoods on the south side of Aurora with several street crossings including busy Montgomery Road. Soon you will cross over Waubonsee Creek. The wetlands along the creek provide a place for migrating waterfowl to rest. Here the trail becomes a bit more rural again with open fields to the south. The trail ends at Hill Avenue just north of Route 34.

On your way back, you may want to visit 200-acre Phillips Park with a large aquatic center, a zoo, and 2 miles of trail on and around Mastodon Lake Island where mastodon bones were discovered while excavating the lake in the 1930s. Phillips Park is .9 mile west of the Virgil Gilman Trail on Ashland Avenue in Aurora. There are sidewalks along Ashland although some have high curbs.

The Virgil Gilman Trail is open daily from 8 a.m. to dusk. Call the Fox Valley Park District at 630-897-0516 for more information. Call the Kane County FPD at 630-466-4182 for information regarding camping at Bliss Woods. Call the Fox Valley Park District at 630-892-1550 for more information on Blackberry Historic Farm-Village.

The trail is open for cross-country skiing in winter.

Silver Springs State Fish and Wildlife Area

Southwest of Aurora and Oswego in Kendall County you will find a 1,314-acre wildlife area along the Fox River. From Silver Springs, the Fox flows southwest for approximately 28 miles through Kendall and LaSalle Counties to Ottowa where it merges with the Illinois River on its way to the Mississippi River. Silver Springs is the farthest south trail site covered in this guidebook. While some distance from much of Chicagoland, this beautiful site is a good place to complete our coverage of the trails of the Fox River Valley. As mentioned earlier in this guidebook, the Fox River Trail will be extended 3 miles south in late 1997 from Mill Street in Montgomery to downtown Oswego in Kendall County. Future plans call for further extension 10 miles southwest through Yorkville and on to Silver Springs.

How to get there:

Take Route 34 southwest from Aurora past Route 47. At Plano, head south on Fox River Road 2 miles to Fox Road. Head east (left). Take either the first or second road to

Silver Springs

Silver Springs State Fish and Wildlife Area

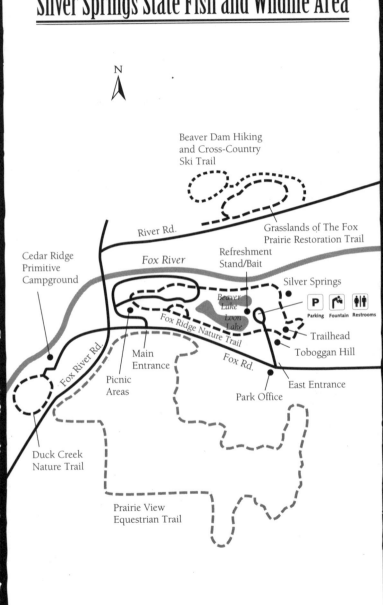

your left to park near the Fox Ridge Nature Trail.

The 4-mile Fox Ridge Nature Trail loops along the south bank of the river, near Beaver and Loon Lakes, and through hilly oak woodlands. Silver Springs gets its name from a pool of clear bubbling water which sparkles like silver on sunny days. You will find the spring along the northeast side of the trail near the east entrance parking area.

Tent camping is available overlooking the Fox River near the 1-mile Duck Creek Nature Trail on the southwest side of the preserve. North of the Fox along River Road are two short trails approximately 1 mile each: the Beaver Dam Hiking and Cross-Country Ski Trail and the Grasslands of the Fox Prairie Restoration Trail. In the wildlife management area south of Fox Road, a 7-mile equestrian trail loops through mostly open fields.

The trails are open for cross-country skiing in winter. Sections of Silver Springs are closed for hunting from September to January each year For more information call the Illinois Department of Natural Resources at 630-553-6297.

Greenway Interconnecting Trails

For those of you who have read any of our other Chicagoland guidebooks, you may note that some of the following is repetitive, but keep reading to learn about exciting plans for new trails in the Fox River Valley and beyond.

For the beginner hiker or biker, 1, 2, or 5-mile trails are sufficient for getting exercise while enjoying nature. But over time many of us want to push on to adventures of longer distances over different paths and trails.

In Kane and McHenry Counties, the rest of Chicagoland, and nationwide, significant progress is being made to interconnect existing park, forest preserve, and other trails. The term greenway identifies a corridor of open land such as an old railroad or utility right-of-way or a waterway that can provide transportation for people and/or wildlife while restoring or preserving the natural environment. Often the greenway contains a trail. The Fox River and its tributaries, such as Nippersink and Tyler

Creeks, and rails-to-trails conversions, such as the Illinois Prairie Path, the Prairie Trail, and the Virgil Gilman Nature Trail are all examples of greenways that offer trails through natural corridors.

Greenways preserve and protect water and air quality and animal life as well as provide recreational opportunities and self-propelled commuting. The Chicagoland greenway system is viewed by many to be the most extensive of any metropolitan area in the country. Greenway initiatives in Boston, New York, Seattle, and other metropolitan areas have also been successful in linking together existing parks, forests, and trails. Given the high cost of land acquisition and the scarcity of available public funds, greenways are also proving to be the most cost-effective way to provide access to open space. Old railroad right-of-ways, river floodplains, utility right-of-ways, and community developments provide opportunities for the creation of new greenways. Often the trail is surrounded by residential neighborhoods, farms, or other development. You may be able to use a greenway trail to visit a park or forest preserve on your bike rather than in your car. These linear park trails are typically much safer than the highways since contending with horses or bicycles is less risky than dealing with cars, buses, and trucks. The purpose of this section is to describe some of the activities underway to provide significantly more trails in the near future within Kane and McHenry Counties and to interconnect with trails originating in the surrounding counties and beyond.

The Northeastern Illinois Planning Commission (NIPC) is partnering with the Openlands Project to coordinate the planning for an interconnected set of trails that will soon cover over 1,000 miles over the six-county Chicago area. Already 500 miles of such regional greenways exist. Linking these trail systems together provides an increasingly interconnected and integrated network of trails similar to our highway and railroad systems.

The Northeastern Illinois Regional Greenways Plan was released in May 1993 with this purpose: "The Greenways Plan creates a vision of an interconnected regionwide network of linear open spaces that will provide benefits to northeastern Illinois—environmental, recreational, economic, aesthetic, and even transportation via trails or waterways."

The plan encompasses Cook, DuPage, Kane, Lake, McHenry, and Will Counties. Greenway opportunities and priorities for development are laid out. The existing greenway network provides an excellent starting point including the major waterways (Chicago, Des Plaines, DuPage, and Fox Rivers), the Lake Michigan shoreline, old railroad routes (the Illinois Prairie Path, the Great Western Trails in DeKalb, Kane and DuPage Counties, the North Shore Path in Lake County, and the Virgil Gilman Trail in Kane County), and even old canals such as the Illinois & Michigan Canal National Heritage Corridor.

Kane County Initiatives

Some of the top priority new greenway trails in Kane County are as follows: a trail along the Blackberry Creek greenway, a Fox River Trail extension in Aurora, an extension of the Great Western Trail east to the Fox River Trail, a trail along the Mill Creek greenway, and a pedestrian/bike path along Randall Road.

Another greenways-related initiative is underway in Kane. The Kane County Division of Transportation has developed the 2020 Transportation Plan—"a comprehensive transportation investment strategy for the next 20-25 years." Pedestrian/bicycle systems are an important element of the plan. New off-road bike and pedestrian bikeways are planned with corridors of interconnected trails running north and south on both sides of the Fox River as well as three east/west corridors. Call the Division of Transportation at 630-584-1170 for more information.

McHenry County Initiatives

Top priorities are a path linking the Prairie Trail to Moraine Hills State Park, completion of the Prairie Trail from Crystal Lake to Ringwood, creation of the H.U.M. Trail (a path along an active railway line from Huntley to Union to Marengo), a five-mile Hebron Trail from the Prairie Trail in Richmond west to Hebron adjacent to the Streets Lake Natural Area, a trail through Lake in the Hills that will help connect the H.U.M. Trail to the Prairie Trail, and the Harvard to Crystal Lake Trail which will be part of the Grand Illinois Trail described in Section 23.

Fox River Trail intersection with Virgil Gilman Trail in Aurora

Greenways Involvement

Many agencies are planning and implementing greenways. These include the Fox Valley Park District, the Illinois Department of Natural Resources, the Kane County Division of Transportation, the Kane County Forest Preserve District, the McHenry County Conservation District, and several communities.

The Regional Greenways plan provides an excellent vision and framework but community and county governments, regional agencies and organizations, federal and state governments, and private sector corporations, land-owners, and interested individuals must play a role in making the plan work. Voice your areas of interest if you'd like to be involved in making the Chicagoland greenways network happen. For more information call NIPC at 312-454-0400 and/or Openlands Project at 312-427-4256.

Interconnecting Trails in Nearby Counties

Greenway trails in nearby counties offer opportunities for extended bike rides and hikes. Several are described in detail in this guidebook i.e. the Illinois Prairie Path in Cook and DuPage Counties, the Boone County Long Prairie Trail, Fermilab trails, and the DeKalb County portion of the Great Western Trail. Many other existing trails can be reached via the Illinois Prairie Path such as several DuPage County Forest Preserve trails and DuPage County's Great Western Trail. Proposed trails in nearby counties will form an ever expanding network of off-road pathways. Some examples include the following:

• Lake County agencies plan to link a West Loop Trail with Moraine Hills State Park; another linkage will cross the Fox River and connect to the Prairie Trail.

• The construction of the Fox River Trail to Oswego in Kendall County is planned for 1997. Future plans call for extension to Silver Springs State Fish & Wildlife Area.

• The 2.5-mile Waubonsee Trail in Oswego will connect with the extension of the Fox River Trail.

• Extension of the Virgil Gilman Trail through Plainfield south to Joliet and northeast to connect with the DuPage River Greenway.

• The 20-mile Centennial Trail from the Chicago Portage National Historic Site in Lyons, Cook County will extend to Lockport in Will County.

• The 38-mile Salt Creek Greenway trail will extend from Ned Brown Forest Preserve in Schaumburg through DuPage County to Brookfield Zoo and on to the Chicago Portage.

Some of these trails will happen soon. Others are probably quite a few years away.

Beyond Chicagoland

In the introduction to his book, *Greenways for America*, Charles E. Little describes the greenway initiatives as a "remarkable citizen-led movement to get us out of our cars and into the landscape—on paths and trails through corridors of green that can link city to country and people to nature from one end of America to the other." Little traces the origins of greenways back to architects such as Fredrich Law Olmsted, the creator of Central Park in New York City. He describes examples both new and old from the Big Sur in California to the Illinois & Michigan Canal National Heritage Corridor to the Hudson

River Valley Greenway in New York. The book is an excellent primer for those interested in furthering the development and interconnection of greenways.

The National Park Service, the American Hiking Society, and a coalition of individuals and many trail support organizations are partnering in an effort called "Trails for All Americans—The National Trails Agenda Project." This effort began in 1988 when the President's Commission on American Outdoors recommended the development of a nationwide network of hiking and jogging trails, bikeways, and bridle paths. Similar to the U.S. Interstate Highway System, planners envision major backbone interstate trails interconnecting with state, county, and local community pathways. The goal is that most Americans would live within 15 minutes of a path that could access this national network.

Eight National Scenic and nine Historic Trails provide the major backbone network. Two examples are described below:

• The Appalachian National Scenic Trail—a completed 2,144-mile trail through the Appalachian Mountains from Katahdin, Maine to Springer Mountain, Georgia.

• The Trail of Tears National Historic Trail—follows the two routes used to move 16,000 Cherokee Indians from Tennessee to Oklahoma, in 1838 and 1839. The water route covers 1,226 miles on the Tennessee, Ohio, Mississippi, and Arkansas Rivers. The 826-mile land route starts in Tennessee, crosses through Kentucky, the southern tip of Illinois, and then Missouri before the sad saga reaches its end in Oklahoma. Development of the entire trail has not yet been completed.

While no National Scenic or Historic Trail runs through Kane or McHenry Counties, a major effort is underway to construct a 500+ miles Grand Illinois Trail that will run through Chicagoland then head west to the Mississippi River north to Galena and back to Chicago. (See Section 23.)

The Grand Illinois will connect with a new national path system, also under development, the American Discovery Trail.

American Discovery Trail

The American Discovery Trail Society and many other agencies and organizations are partnering in the development of a 6,300-mile

American Discovery Trail (ADT). Three thousand five hundred miles of trails consisting of both on and off-road routes are already marked.

From the trailhead near the Atlantic Ocean at the Cape Henlopen State Park in Delaware to the Pacific Ocean at the Point Reyes National Seashore in California, the ADT will run through urban and remote areas in 15 states and Washington D. C. Through the mid-western states including Illinois, there will be both a northern and a southern route forming a gigantic loop from Cincinnati to Denver. Open to hikers, bicyclists, and equestrians, the ADT will connect to six national scenic trails and ten national historic trails as well as many regional and local trail systems such as ours here in Chicagoland. In northern Illinois, the ADT includes the I & M Canal State Trail, the Hennepin Canal State Trail, and the Old Plank Road Trail, currently under development. Trail users will truly be able to sample the diversity of America from the seashores to the deserts, to the mountains to the prairies, to the rivers, and streams, to the towns and cities along the way. Contact the American Discovery Trail Society at 510-283-6800 for more information.

Trail User Support

Unfortunately, recent federal budget cutting initiatives in Washington have negatively impacted the progress of trails development. Some of the planned trail systems mentioned above will be delayed or perhaps never built. If you are interested in seeing the expansion of trails and off-road hiking and bicycling paths, voice your opinions to local, state, and federal government representatives particularly your U. S. House of Representatives legislators.

The Grand Illinois Trail

So you say you want to take a really long hike or bike ride! The Illinois Department of Natural Resources (IDNR) is partnering with many other agencies and organizations to develop one nearby. The Grand Illinois Trail consists of a 475-mile circular loop from Navy Pier in Chicago past Starved Rock State Park to the Mississippi River via the Illinois & Michigan and the Hennepin Canal State Trails, then north along the Great River Trail to Savanna and Mississippi Palisades State Park, continue along The Northwest Hills Trail in Jo Daviess County to Galena then back to Chicago through the other counties bordering Wisconsin.

Additional trail opportunities relating to the Grand Illinois Trail will include parts of the existing Fox River Trail, Illinois Prairie Path, and the Prairie Trail as well as the Des Plaines River Trail in Lake and Cook Counties, the Centennial and Old Plank Road Trail in Cook and Will Counties, and other existing and proposed on- and off-road routes.

In total, the Grand Illinois Trail system will contain 500+ miles of rail trails, bike paths, canal tow paths, and greenways along with

The Grand Illinois Trail

street routes and lightly traveled township and county roads as it traverses the state. Camping and lodging is available along the way. Hikers, bicyclists, equestrians and other trail users will be able to see parts of the state they probably have never visited before. Trail enthusiasts will be able to enjoy nearby adventure vacations taking on the entire trail in a single effort or more likely completing one segment at a time.

Existing trails such as the 61-mile Illinois & Michigan Canal State Trail in Will, Grundy, and La Salle Counties will be part of the Grand Illinois. In fact, approximately 200 miles of trail are already in place. Projects totaling 90 miles are funded for construction or improvement. In addition, at least for now, about 185 miles are proposed along local roads or streets. The goal is to complete the Grand Illinois Trail by the year 2000. While it will take time and a major effort by the involved agencies to construct, the Grand Illinois Trail will be an outstanding asset to trail users as well as the communities along the way.

In spring of 1996, Kandee Haertel, President of the Illinois Trailriders Association, and Mike Ulm, State Director of the Illinois Rails-to-Trails Conservancy, had a "Grand Adventure". These trailblazers were the first to make their way around the Grand Illinois Trail. Using bicycles, horses, in-line skates, a canoe, as well as foot power, Kandee and Mike helped promote and draw attention to the Grand Illinois. While much of their route was on-road in 1996, as each year passes, more and more of the Grand Illinois route will include off-road trails and bike paths.

If you are interested in finding out more, call the Grand Illinois Trail Coordinator at 815-732-9072 or the IDNR Division of Planning at 815-782-3715.

Appendices

Attractions

Algonquin
Algonquin Princess Paddleboat
20 W. Algonquin Road (847) 658-3660

Dundee
Haeger Potteries
7 Maiden Lane (847) 426-3441

Elgin
Civic Center Plaza/Hemmens
Cultural Center
150 Dexter Court (847) 697-3616

Grand Victoria Riverboat Casino
250 S. Grove Avenue (847) 468-7000

Trout Park
Rt. 25 & I-90 (847) 931-6120

South Elgin
Blackhawk Forest Preserve
35W003 Rt. 31 (847) 741-7883

Fox River Trolley Museum
Rt. 31 (847) 697-4676

St. Charles
Century Corners Shopping District
Main Street & 2nd Avenue

Durant-Peterson House/Sholes School
LeRoy Oakes Forest Preserve
(630) 377-6424 or (630) 377-6161

River View Miniature Golf Pottawatomie Park
2 North Avenue (630) 584-1028

Old St. Charles Shopping District
Main & Third Streets

Paddlewheel Riverboat Excursions
2 North Avenue (630) 584-2334

Piano Factory Outlet Mall
410 S. First Street (630) 584-2099

Tekakwitha Woods Forest Preserve
and Nature Center
35W076 Villa Marie Road
(847) 741-8350

Geneva
Geneva Historical Museum
400 Wheeler Drive (630) 232-4951

Historic Geneva Shopping District
Rts. 31 & 38 (630) 232-6060

Batavia
Batavia Depot Museum
155 Houston Street
(630) 406-5274

Batavia Riverwalk
Houston Street & Island Avenue
(630) 879-5235

Fermi National Accelerator Laboratory
Kirk & Wilson Streets (630) 840-3351

Funway Entertainment Center
Rt. 25 (630) 879-8717

Hall Quarry Beach
Union & Water Streets
(630) 406-5275

North Aurora
North Aurora Off-Track Betting Facility
230 S. Lincolnway (Rt. 31)
(630) 892-6200

Aurora
Aurora Historical Society and
Aurora Public Arts Commission
20 E. Downer Place (630) 906-0650

Aurora Regional Fire Museum
53 N. Broadway (630) 892-1572

Blackberry Historical Farm-Village
W. Galena Blvd. & Barnes Road
(630)-892-1550

Hollywood Casino-Aurora
One New York St. Bridge (630) 801-1234

Michael Jordan Golf Center
4523 Michael Jordan Drive (630) 851-0023

Paramount Arts Centre
23 E. Galena Blvd. (630) 896-6666

Phillips Park/Aquatic Center
Smith Blvd. at Ray Moses Drive
(630) 898-7228

SciTech Interactive Science and
Technology Center
18 W. Benton Street (630) 859-3434

Walter Payton's Roundhouse Complex
205 N. Broadway (630) 264-BREW

LaFox
Garfield Farm Museum
Garfield Road and Rt. 38 (630) 584-8485

Sugar Grove
Waubonsee Community College
Rt. 47 at Harter Road (630) 466-4811

Bike/Skate
Service & Rental

Crystal Lake
Crystal Lake Ski & Bike
905A Pyott Road (815) 455-5450

Algonquin
Prairie Trail Bike Shop
315 Railroad (847) 658-1154

East Dundee
Dundee Township Tourist Center, Inc.
"The Depot", 319 N. River Street
(847) 426-2255
(air pump, tools, patch kits available)

South Elgin
Village Peddler
300 S. Route 31 (LaFox)
(847) 741-5938

St. Charles
The Bike Rack
37W610 Campton Hills Road
(630) 584-6588

Fox River Schwinn
1717 W. Main Street
(630) 377-2453

Geneva
Mill Race Cyclery
11 E. State Street (630) 232-2833
(rentals available)

Batavia
Fox River Outdoor Store
Rt. 25 & Wilson Street (630) 406-0020

North Aurora
Fox River Schwinn
19 S. Lincolnway (Rt. 31)
(630) 897-6200 (rentals available)

Pedal & Spoke
157 S. Lincolnway (Rt. 31)
(630) 892-1010 (rentals available)

Aurora
The Wheel Shop
47 E. Illinois Avenue
(630) 896-2400 (rentals available)

Oswego
Oswego Cycle
Rt. 25 and Rt. 34
(630) 554-0309 (rentals available)

First Aid
Call 911 for emergencies
(*911 for cellular phones)

East Dundee
Dundee Township Tourist Center, Inc.
"The Depot" 319 N. River Street
(847) 426-2255

Elgin
Sherman Hospital
934 Center Street (847) 742-9800

Geneva
Delnor Community Hospital
300 Randall Road (630) 208-3000

Batavia
Batavia Police Department
100 N. Island Avenue (630) 879-2840

North Aurora
North Aurora Police Department
25 E. State Street (630) 897-8705

Aurora
Aurora Police Department
350 N. River Street (630) 859-1700

Dreyer Medical Clinic
1870 W. Galena Blvd. (630) 859-6700

Mercy Center for Healthcare Services
1325 N. Highland (630) 859-2222

Rush-Copley Medical Center
2000 Odgen Avenue (630) 978-6200

Food/Beverage

Algonquin
Golden Eagle Ice Cream & Sandwich
Parlor, 301 S. Main (847) 658-3311

Port Edward Restaurant
20 W. Algonquin (Rt. 62)
(847) 658-5441

Reese's Restaurant
205 S. Main (847) 658-8550

East Dundee
Dundee Dairy Queen
15 E. Main (847) 428-2443

Piece-A-Cake Bakery
304 N. River Street (847) 836-6703

Elgin
Al's Cafe & Creamery
43 DuPage Ct. (847) 742-1180

Alessandra's Sweet Shoppe
Grove & Highland Ave. (847) 697-7723

Facaccia's Restaurant
50 N. Spring Street (847) 695-2181

Grand Victoria Riverboat Casino
250 S. Grove Avenue (847) 468-7000

Jalapeño's Restaurant
7 Clock Tower Plaza (847) 468-9445

Prairie Rock Brewing Company
127 S. Grove Avenue (847) 622-8888

Seattle Mountain Coffee Company
Grove & Highland Ave. (847) 695-3595

St. Charles
Blue Goose Super Market (Deli)
164 S. 1st Street (630) 584-0900

Twisters/Colonial
110 N. 3rd Street (630) 584-9878

Erik & Me
1 W. Illinois Street (630) 443-6210

Filling Station Antique Eatery
300 W. Main Street (630) 584-4414

First Avenue Cafe
15 E. Main Street (630) 513-0239

The Manor Restaurant
1 W. Main St. (630) 584-2469

Salerno's on the Fox
320 N. 2nd Street (630) 584-7900

Starbuck's
101 E. Main Street (630) 443-0990

Town House Cafe (Century Corners)
105 N. 2nd Avenue (630) 584-8603

The Upper Crust
(at Piano Factory Outlet Mall)
410 S. First Street (630) 584-3220

Batavia
Baskin Robbins, Batavia Meat Market/
Deli, European Pastries, Maria's Pizza,
Mama Rosa's Pizzeria, Parsley & Basil's
Island Avenue

East China Inn
Shumway Avenue (630) 879-7676

North Aurora
A & W Family Restaurant
113 S. Lincolnway (Rt. 31)
(630) 844-9393

Hardee's Restaurant
411 S. Lincolnway (Rt. 31)
(630) 264-1401

Harner's Bakery & Restaurant
10 W. State Street (630) 892-4400

Aurora
America's Brewpub
205 N. Broadway (630) 264-BREW

Colonial Cafe
1961 W.Galena Blvd. (630) 844-2444

McDonald's
1023 N. Lake Street

Oberweis Dairy Store
945 N. Lake Street (630) 897-6600

Pepe's Mexican Restaurant
749 N. Lake Street (630) 844-2000

Pizza Hut
701 N. Lake Street (630) 897-8060

Reuland's Food Service
115 Oak Street (630) 859-2877

Wasco
Collins General Store
40W514 Rt. 64 (630) 377-3911

Silverado
41W379 Rt. 64 (630) 513-8335

Wasco Inn
40W301 Rt. 64 (630) 584-7377

Information

Dundee Township Tourist Center, Inc.
"The Depot" 319 N. River St., East Dundee
(847) 426-2255

Elgin Area Convention & Visitors Bureau
77 Riverside Drive (847) 695-7540

Grand Victoria Riverboat Casino
250 S. Grove Avenue, Elgin (847) 468-7000

St. Charles Convention & Visitors Bureau
311 N. Second Street (630) 377-6161

Geneva Chamber of Commerce
8 S. Third Street (630) 232-6060

Batavia Chamber of Commerce
100 N. Island Avenue (630) 879-7134

Aurora Area Convention
& Tourism Council
44 W. Downer Pl. (630) 897-5581

Fox Valley Park District (630) 897-0516

Sycamore Chamber of Commerce
206 W. State Street (815) 895-3456

Village of **North Aurora**
(708) 897-8551

Village of **Sugar Grove**
(708) 466-5407

Lodging

Elgin
Days Inn
1585 Dundee Avenue (847) 695-2100

Elgin Budgetel Inn
500 Toll Gate Road (847) 931-4800

Hampton Inn
405 Airport Road (847) 931-1940

Holiday Inn Holidome
345 W. River Road. (847) 695-5000

Super 8
435 Airport Road. (847) 697-8828

St. Charles
Best Western Inn of St. Charles
1635 E. Main St. (630) 584-4550

Days Inn
100 S. Tyler Road (630) 513-6500

Econo Lodge
1600 E. Main St. (630) 584-5300

Hotel Baker
100 W. Main St. (630) 584-2100
(Opening Fall of 1997)

Pheasant Run Resort &
Convention Center
4051 E. Main St. (630) 584-6300

Super 8 of St. Charles
1520 E. Main St. (630) 377-8388

Geneva
The Herrington
15 S. River Lane (630) 208-7433

Oscar Swan Inn
1800 W. State Street (630) 232-0173

Batavia
Villa Batavia
1430 S. Batavia Ave. (630) 406-8182

North Aurora
Howard Johnson
306 S. Lincolnway (630) 892-6481

Aurora
Best Western Fox Valley Inn
2450 N. Farnsworth Ave.
(630) 851-2000

Comfort Inn Aurora
4005 Gabrielle Lane (630) 820-3400

Comfort Suites City Center
111 N. Broadway (630) 896-2800

Motel 6
2380 N. Farnsworth Avenue
(630) 851-3600

Riverwalk Inn
77 S. Stolp Ave. (630) 892-0001

Yorkville
Super 8
1510 N. Bridge St. (Rt. 47)
(630) 553-1634

Bed & Breakfasts

Algonquin
Victorian Rose Garden
314 Washington Street (847) 854-9667

West Dundee
Ironhedge Inn
305 Oregon Avenue (847) 426-7777

St. Charles
Charleston Guest House
612 W. Main St. (630) 377-1277

Yorkville
Fox and Hounds Bed and Breakfast
201 E. Jackson St. (630) 553-1369

Silver Key Bed and Breakfast
507 W. Ridge St. (800) 246-3384

Oswego
Gilbert Gaylord House
1542 Plainfield Rd. (630) 554-1865

Wal-Oak Bed and Breakfast
224 Chicago Road (630) 554-9625

Information provided by:
Aurora Area Convention and Tourism
Council (800) 477-4369

Elgin Area Convention and
Visitors Bureau (800) 217-5362

St. Charles Convention and
Visitors Bureau (800) 777-4373

Calendar of Events

Each event is shown under the month scheduled at time of publication. Call for more specific information.

January

Candlelight Skiing, various sites
McHenry County Conservation District
815-678-4431

Winterfest, Volo Bog
Illinois Department of Natural Resources
815-344-1294

February

Candlelight Skiing, various sites
McHenry County Conservation District
815-678-4431

Midwest Bicycle Show
Rosemont
847-202-0795

March

Maple Sugaring, Coral Woods
McHenry County Conservation District
815-678-4421

Red Oak Maple Syrup Festival
Fox Valley Park District
630-897-1808

Maple Sugaring
Tekakwitha Woods Nature Center, St. Charles
Kane County Forest Preserve District
847-741-8350

April

Spring Bird Walks
Bliss Woods, Sugar Grove
Kane County Forest Preserve District
April/May
847-741-8350

Arbor Day Habitat Restoration Event
Burnidge Forest Preserve, Elgin
Kane County Forest Preserve District
847-741-9798

Ecofest, Volo Bog
Illinois Dept. of Natural Resources
815-344-1294

Spring Wildflower Walks
Johnson's Mound, Elburn
Kane County Forest Preserve District
April/May
847-741-8350

Spring Bird Walks
Nelson Lake Marsh, Batavia
Kane County Forest Preserve District
April/May
847-741-8350

Spring Bird and Wildflower Walks
Tekakwitha Woods, St. Charles
Kane County Forest Preserve District
April/May
847-741-8350

May

Bike to Work Week
Chicagoland Bicycle Federation
312-42-PEDAL

Elgin Valley Fox Trot
5K/10K Runs/2 mile walk, City of Elgin
847-931-6120

Laracol
21/40/62 metric century bike rides, St. Charles
Association of Late-Deafened Adults
630-443-0314

Pizza Ride
17, 33, 50, 74M bike rides, Elgin
Windy City Sports
312-421-6827

Prairie Pedal
20/40/60 M bike rides/5M family ride
Prairie Crossing, Grayslake
847-548-5989

Silver Springs 60
Yorkville
Aurora Bicycle Club
708-892-1010

Wheels & Heels
5K run, bike-a-thon, 2K family nature walk
Fermilab/ Batavia, American Cancer Society
800-942-6985

June

Bicycle Club of Lake County Ramble
30, 60, 80, 100 M rides, Wauconda
847-604-0520

Crystal Lake Park District Triathlon
1K swim, 30K bike, 8.5K run, Crystal Lake
815-459-0680

Fox Fest
Power Boat Races
McCullough Park, Aurora
630-892-8811

Harvard Milk Run
2M, 10K runs, Harvard
815-943-4614

Journey for Sight
25, 45, 62M bike rides
Waubonsee Community College,
Sugar Grove
Aurora Evening Lions Club
630-896-2474

Day In The Country Antique Sale
Leroy Oaks Forest Preserve, St. Charles
Kane County Forest Preserve District
630-377-6424

Lake Tour Bike Trek
100, 150 M bike rides
Crystal Lake to Lake Geneva
American Lung Association
630-469-2400

Mid-America Canoe Race
Elgin to Aurora
630-859-8606

Pride of the Fox River
Geneva
630-377-6161

Prairie Fest
1M, 5K runs, Oswego
630-554-1010

Swedish Days Ride
25/50/75/100 M rides
American Legion, Wasco
Fox Valley Bicycle Club
630-584-7353

Udder Century
10/31/50/62/100M rides, McHenry County
McHenry County Bicycle Club
815-477-6858 or 708-442-1188

July

Metro-Metric Invitational
The Wizard of Oswego
22, 40, 62, 100 M bike rides
Oswego, Elmhurst Bicycle Club
630-415-BIKE

Mid-Summer Classic Triathlon
1K swim, 30K bike, 8.5K run, Crystal Lake
Crystal Lake Park Foundation
and Special Recreation Foundation
815-459-0680

Summer Concert, Volo Bog
Illinois Department of Natural Resources
815-344-1294

5K Run at Blackberry Farm
Fox Valley Park District, Aurora
630-859-8606

August

Art on the Fox
Downtown Aurora
630-906-0654

Coon Creek Classic
10K race, 2K fun run, Hampshire
847-683-2690

Elgin Fine Arts Festival
Wing Park, Elgin
847-931-6120

Fox Valley Folk Festival
Labor Day Weekend, Geneva
630-232-4542

I Tried A Triathlon
250 yd. swim, 10K bike, 2.1M run, Oswego
630-554-1010

North Aurora Days
5K, 10K Runs, North Aurora
630-897-8551

September

Cardunal Fall Ride
20 M ride, East Dundee
Dundee Bicycle Club
847-622-4100

Festival of the Vine
Geneva
630-232-6060

Harmon Hundred
30/62/100 M rides, Wauconda
Wheeling Wheelmen
847-520-5010

Woodstock Challenge
2M, 10K runs, Woodstock
815-338-4363

October

The Fox Chase
5K run, 1/4 and 1 mile youth runs
Fox River Grove
Fox River Grove Recreational Council
847-639-9523

Pumpkin Pedal Bike Ride for the Special
Olympics
10, 20, 40, 62 M, Geneva
630-377-7250

Scarecrow Festival
St. Charles
630-377-6161

Sycamore Pumpkin Festival
10 K road race, Sycamore
815-895-5161

Haunted Halloween Hike & Campfire
Tekakwitha Woods Nature Center, St.
Charles
Kane County Forest Preserve District
847-741-8350

Trail of History, Glacial Park
McHenry County Conservation District
815-678-4431

Volunteer Prairie Seed Harvest
Fermilab, Batavia
630-840-3351

November

Gobbler Hobbler
1M, 10K runs, Oswego
630-554-1010

December

Candlelight Open House
Durant House- Pioneer Sholes School
LeRoy Oakes Forest Preserve, St. Charles
Kane County Forest Preserve District
630-377-6424

Fox River Outdoor Store Reindeer Romp
5K, run, walk, Batavia
630-406-0020

Organizations

Bicycle Clubs

Aurora Bicycle Club
P. O. Box 972
Aurora, IL 60507
708-892-1010

Chicagoland Bicycle Federation
417 S. Dearborn, Suite 1000
Chicago, IL 60605
312-42-PEDAL

Dundee Bicycle Club
319 N. River Street
East Dundee, IL 60118
847-622-4100

Fox Valley Bicycle Club
P. O. Box 1073
St. Charles, IL 60174
630-584-7353

League of Illinois Bicyclists
417 S. Dearborn, Suite 1000
Chicago, IL 60605
312-42-PEDAL

McHenry County Bicycle Club
P. O. Box 917
Crystal Lake, IL 60014
815-477-6858

Recreation for Individuals Dedicated
to the Environment (RIDE)
Suite 1700, 208 S. LaSalle Street
Chicago, IL 60604
312-853-2820

Trail Users Rights Foundation (TURF)
P. O. Box 403
Summit, IL 60501
847-470-4266

Environmental

Fermilab Prairie Project Volunteers
630-840-3351

Kane County Natural Area Volunteers
719 Batavia Avenue, Bldg. G
Geneva, IL 60134
630-232-5880

Illinois Ornithological Society
P. O. Box 1971
Evanston, IL 60204
847-566-4846

McHenry County Defenders
132 Cass Street
Woodstock, IL 60098
815-338-0393

McHenry County Chapter of the
Illinois Audubon Society
P. O. Box 67
Woodstock, IL 60098
217-446-5085

Sierra Club, Illinois Chapter
One N. LaSalle Street, Suite 4242
Chicago, IL 60602
(Includes the Valley of the Fox
Group/Kane County and The
Blackhawk Group/McHenry County)
312-251-1680

The Friends of Volo Bog
28478 W. Brandenburg Road
Ingleside, IL 60041
815-344-1294

The Nature Conservancy, Illinois Field Office
Volunteer Stewardship Office
8 S. Michigan, Suite 900
Chicago, IL 60603
312-346-8166

Hiking and Walking

American Hiking Society
P. O. Box 20160
Washington, D. C. 20041
301-565-6704

Forest Trails Hiking Club
714 W. Waveland Avenue
Chicago, IL 60613
312-248-8091

Trails

The Illinois Prairie Path
P. O. Box 1086
Wheaton, IL 60189
630-752-0120

Illinois Chapter of the Rails-to-Trails Conservancy
319 W. Cook Street,
Springfield, IL 62704
217-789-4782

Illinois Trailriders (a statewide equestrian group)
5765 Virginia
Clarendon Hills, IL 60514
630-887-8542

Bibliography

Books

The Complete Guide to America's National Parks. National Park Foundation. 1992-93 Edition.

Greenways for America. Little, Charles E. Johns Hopkins University Press. 1990.

Kane County Wild Plants & Natural Areas, 2nd Edition, Dick Young, Kane County Forest Preserve District, 1994.

Other Publications

Origin and Evolution of Illinois Counties. Printed by authority of the State of Illinois. April, 1992.

Prehistoric People in McHenry County, an archaeological survey of McHenry County, The McHenry County Conservation District, 1988.

State of The Greenways Report. Prepared by Northeastern Illinois Planning Commission and Openlands Project. July, 1994.

The Northeastern Illinois Regional Greenways Plan. Developed by the Northeastern Illinois Planning Commission and Openlands Project. May, 1993.

Trails for all Americans—The Report of the National Trails Agenda Project. Submitted by American Trails to the National Park Service. Summer, 1990.

About The Team

Author/publisher, Jim Hochgesang, is a hiking and biking enthusiast. Jim and his wife, Sandy, started a small self-publishing company, Roots & Wings, in spring of 1993. Since then a series of four regional hiking and biking guidebooks have been published. Our other three books cover Cook, DuPage, and Lake Counties. Roots & Wings guidebooks can be found in over 250 Chicagoland stores.

Sheryl DeVore, who edited and added natural history information to all our guidebooks, has won many first place national and regional awards for her environment and nature writing. A volunteer for the Lake County Forest Preserves, Sheryl is also chief editor of Meadowlark, A Journal of Illinois Birds as well as an author of many nature-related articles in national magazines. Sheryl is an ardent birder and hiker.

Melanie Lawson is a designer and calligrapher living and working in the Chicago area. She is also an avid hiker.

Comments from Our Customers

Your comments related to this guidebook are very much appreciated for our use in improving future issues.

_____

_____

_____

_____

We are also considering publishing other hiking/biking guidebooks. Would you be interested in the following?

	Level of Interest		
	High	**Medium**	**Low**
• Hiking & Biking the I & M Canal National Heritage Corridor	☐	☐	☐
• Hiking & Biking in Will and Kendall Counties, Illinois	☐	☐	☐
• Hiking & Biking in Door County, Wisconsin	☐	☐	☐
• Hiking & Biking in Southeastern Wisconsin	☐	☐	☐

We will be happy to include you on our mailing list to announce any upcoming products.

Name _____

Address _____

City, State, Zip Code _____

Thanks for your input.

Order Form

Send _____ copy/copies of Roots & Wings Hiking & Biking guidebooks to the following address:

Name _____

Address _____

City, State, Zip Code _____

Please enclose a personal check for the total amount made payable to Roots & Wings, P.O. Box 167, Lake Forest, Illinois, 60045. Thank you for your order!

_____ books @ $12.95 = _____	*Hiking & Biking in Cook County, Illinois*	
_____ books @ $11.95 = _____	*Hiking & Biking in DuPage County, Illinois*	
_____ books @ $12.95 = _____	*Hiking & Biking in The Fox River Valley*	
_____ books @ $12.95 = _____	*Hiking & Biking in Lake County, Illinois* 2nd Edition **(Available 7/97)**	

Subtotal   = _____

Illinois Residents Add
Sales Tax @ 6.5%   = _____

Shipping and Handling   = ___$1.95___

Total   = _____

Also you may buy additional copies of these guidebooks at bookstores, bicycle shops, nature stores, and outfitters as well as other merchants throughout Chicagoland.